W9-AWO-111

Integrity

Integrity

Good People, Bad Choices,
and Life Lessons from
the White House

Egil "Bud" Krogh

with
Matthew Krogh

PublicAffairs™
New York

Copyright © 2007 by Egil Krogh and Matthew Krogh

Published in the United States by PublicAffairs™, a member of the Perseus
Books Group.

All rights reserved.

No part of this book may be reproduced in any manner whatsoever without
written permission except in the case of brief quotations embodied in critical
articles and reviews. For information, address PublicAffairs, 250 West 57th
Street, Suite 1321, New York, NY 10107.

Public Affairs books are available at special discounts for bulk purchases in
the U.S. by corporations, institutions, and other organizations. For more
information, please contact the Special Markets Department at the Perseus
Books Group, 2300 Chestnut Street, Suite 200, Philadelphia, PA 19103, or
call (800) 255-1514, or email special.markets@perseusbooks.com.

Library of Congress Cataloging-in-Publication Data
Krogh, Egil, 1939-
   Integrity : good people, bad choices, and life lessons from the
White House / by Egil "Bud" Krogh, with Matthew Krogh.
      p. cm.
   Includes index.
   ISBN-13: 978-1-58648-467-5
   ISBN-10: 1-58648-467-2
   1. Krogh, Egil, 1939- 2. Watergate Affair, 1972-1974—
Personal narratives. 3. United States—Politics and government—
1969-1974 4. Nixon, Richard M. (Richard Milhous), 1913-1994.
I. Krogh, Matthew D. II. Title.
   E860.K77 2007
   973.924092—dc22
   [B]

                                                              2007022104

First Edition

To those who deserved better,
this book is offered as an apology,
an explanation, and a way to keep
integrity in the forefront of decisionmaking.

Contents

Contents

Foreword

Daniel Ellsberg

In July 1958, Congress passed a code of ethics for government service. By law, it was supposed to be displayed somewhere within every federal office, but after a dozen years as a consultant to or employee of federal departments, I saw it for the first time in 1971 on an office wall in La Tuna Federal Correction Facility in New Mexico.

I was there to visit a prisoner named Randy Kehler to let him know that his noncooperation with the Vietnam-era draft had not been without positive consequences. Soon after I heard him describe his decision in August 1969, I had copied the seven thousand pages of a top-secret history of decisionmaking in Vietnam from my safe at the Rand Corporation and given it to the Senate Foreign Relations Committee. Randy had just entered prison at that point. I told him in the spring of '71, in the visitors' center in La Tuna, that although Senator William Fulbright had finally decided against taking the political risk of introducing the secret study in hearings—Secretary of Defense Melvin Laird having refused to give it to him officially, even on a classified basis—and other senators having likewise backed off after initial interest, I was determined to get the truth out by other means, perhaps through a newspaper. I wanted Randy to know that his example was still at work.

I was also interested in hearing his account of prison life, since I expected to be living in a similar institution before long. (It occurred to me the next day that the visitors' center might well have been wired, and I crossed my fingers, but apparently it wasn't: the *New York Times* began publishing the Pentagon Papers a few months later.)

While I waited in an outer office to be led into the visitors' center, I noticed a large government regulation mounted under glass on the wall, the "Code of Ethics for Government Service." It listed ten principles, like commandments. The first one was: "Put loyalty to the highest moral principles and to country above loyalty to persons, party, or Government department."

I had never seen an official statement quite like that, with those specifics; I could hardly imagine it as a government pronouncement. (To be sure, it emerged from the legislative branch, not the executive, but it had been signed by President Eisenhower.) My first thought, with a start of recognition, was: *That's what I've just done. It's what I'm doing now, at last.* Adhering to that principle was, somewhat ironically, why I would be joining Randy Kehler in prison before long. Yet it was also, it appeared, what Congress had prescribed for me from the very month, July 1958, I had started work on a government contract at the Rand Corporation. What I now recognized was that as a practical matter, without thinking about it, I had broken this commandment repeatedly in the decade that followed, which included a year as a Defense Department official and two years with the State Department in Vietnam before I came back to Rand as a researcher and government consultant. So had most of my colleagues. So, as the following memoir recounts, Egil Krogh was about to do.

The first part of the code of ethics, defining where highest loyalty was to go for a government employee, could be regarded as somewhat vague and subjective, but the last half of the statement was not, nor was the order of priority between the two parts. By 1971, I could recognize that this seemingly unobjectionable, almost truistic proposition—probably it would look self-evident to someone with less experience with the executive branch—if taken seriously, radically challenged the actual operating ethics of the bureaucracy. Loyalty to "persons" (your bosses and teammates, and above all the president), to "party" (for political appointees), to "Government department"—that was the air you breathed, the first premise of your position and the trust placed in you. Reminders of the paramount importance of these loyalties, the pointing of negative and positive examples to warn and inspire you, were daily matters.

The very notion that one should, not just as lip service to some abstraction but as a practical matter affecting your official performance, recognize and take into account loyalty to something, anything, that was higher than any of these obligations—that thought was totally foreign to the internalized and socially enforced ethical code of an executive official. It was simply not thinkable. This was true even though the sworn, declared object of loyalty required of every government official was not any of these but solely the Constitution.

Here is the oath of office required by law for every military officer and civilian official: "I do solemnly swear [or affirm] that I will support and defend the Constitution of the United States against all enemies, foreign and domestic; that I will bear true faith and allegiance to the same; that I take this obligation freely, without any mental reservation or purpose of evasion; and that I will well and faithfully discharge the duties of the office on which I am about to enter. So help me God." The Constitution: period.

Egil Krogh and I had each taken this oath more than once: I as a Marine officer, later as an official in the Departments of Defense and State; he in the Navy and later in the White House and

Department of Transportation. But speaking for myself, I don't recall that it ever occurred to me that I was taking on obligations to the Constitution that might contradict—let alone take precedence over—the demands of a cabinet secretary or the president. Even if I had earlier seen the Code of Ethics, whose second principle was "Uphold the Constitution, laws, and legal regulations of the United States . . . and never be a party to their evasion," I would not have been at all alert before the late sixties to the potential conflict in those elements: the possibility that obeying such regulations as the secrecy rules and agreements might make me party to evasions of the Constitution and laws by the president himself and his subordinates, my superiors. But by the spring of 1971, when I finally read that code on the wall of a prison in New Mexico, that possibility was known to me as a reality.

By then I had experienced as an official—and read in the Pentagon Papers history going back to 1945—that a succession of presidents had violated their own presidential oaths of office "to preserve, protect and defend the Constitution" by usurping the war powers assigned constitutionally to Congress and by deceiving Congress (and the electorate) systematically about their policies in Vietnam. (I didn't know it at the time, but Presidents Johnson and Nixon had also been violating domestic laws as well as the Fourth Amendment by authorizing warrantless wiretaps—as George W. Bush has now been doing for more than five years, along with illegal domestic surveillance by the CIA.) In serving several of them unquestioningly and by keeping all their secrets, even when I knew the Congress and public were being lied to, I had been violating my own oath to uphold the Constitution—as had all of my many colleagues who were knowledgeable about the deceptions. And as Egil Krogh was shortly to do—just months after my visit with Randy Kehler—when President

Nixon made him co-chair of the self-named White House Plumbers with the mission of stopping further leaks, especially by me, after the publication of the Pentagon Papers.

Of course, Krogh—Bud, as I've come to know him as a friend—didn't see his actions in that light at the time, any more than I had, or my associates. As he explains in this book—speaking I would say for most of us in the executive branch—invocation by the president of the needs of "national security" made constraints of domestic laws and even the Constitution inoperative: irrelevant in his own eyes, as in the president's, to what had to be done. In the area of national security at least, few of us while we were serving would have seen a problem with President Nixon's later formulation (speaking of the burglary of my doctor's office that Egil Krogh had directed in his name): "When the president does it, it's not illegal." So Bud's immediate boss, John Ehrlichman—his close friend and mentor, also a lawyer and the president's domestic counsel—believed when he authorized the break-in, and continued to believe after he, like Bud, but without pleading guilty, had gone to prison for it. So Nixon (spared from the risk of prison by a pardon) thought to the end of his life.

But Bud Krogh came to see it differently. Months into his indictment, faced with the rejection by his judge of the justification of national security that he had relied on in his own mind up until then for his feeling of innocence, he suddenly came to realize that he agreed with the judge: that his actions had not been justified, that they amounted not only to crimes but to violations of constitutional rights and principles that were fundamental to our form of government and that deserved protection. Like so many others, like myself earlier, he had put personal loyalties above the loyalty owed the Constitution.

Unlike many others, Bud had the extraordinary courage and integrity—perhaps it should not be extraordinary, but it is—not only to see that and regret it, but to accept the implications of his conclusion for his life. He proceeded to change his plea to guilty, to reject any notion of a presidential pardon or a deal that would spare him jail time, and to accept his prison sentence. He has always acted as a patriot, but never more so than by honoring his oath in this fashion.

I would be glad—in current circumstances above all—if every public servant were to read and learn from this memoir. Our nation and our constitutional democracy, presently in danger, would be safer for it.

Introduction

During seven weeks of secret work in 1971, my group and I undermined the foundations of Richard Nixon's presidency. At that time, David Young and I codirected the "Plumbers," a secret White House group more formally known as the Special Investigations Unit, or SIU. We had been tasked by the president himself with stopping leaks of top-secret information related to the Vietnam War, the Strategic Arms Limitation Talks (SALT), and other sensitive foreign policy operations. We believed then that these leaks constituted a national security crisis and needed to be plugged at all costs. But we were wrong, and the price paid by the country was too high.

For thirty-five years I have pondered the reasons why I committed a serious crime as codirector of the Plumbers. Our seven-week investigation in 1971 targeted what we believed to be a serious national security threat, Dr. Daniel Ellsberg's leak of the top-secret Pentagon Papers to the *New York Times*, and culminated in the break-in of the office of his psychiatrist, Dr. Lewis Fielding. This crime and several others that followed, including the Watergate break-in and the illegal efforts to cover it up, eventually doomed the Nixon presidency. The break-in and burglary of Dr. Fielding's office was the seminal event in the chain of events that led to Nixon's resignation on August 8, 1974.

The seven-week period in 1971 that doomed the Nixon presidency was not the only cause of that political tragedy, but the burglary set a precedent that two members of the Plumbers could rely on when planning and executing the Watergate break-in of 1972. They knew that under certain circumstances the White House staff would tolerate an illegal act to obtain information. Later, during the intensive Watergate investigations, a major reason for the cover-up by President Nixon and former members of his staff was to prevent investigators from discovering information about the 1971 crime. Extreme illegal acts were undertaken to prevent this discovery, including perjury, obstruction of justice, and the payment of hush money to the perpetrators of the 1971 crime to keep them from revealing it during the Watergate investigation. Several members of Nixon's top staff feared that discovery of the 1971 events would imperil them and the president himself. Former attorney general John Mitchell, when apprised in 1972 of what had happened in 1971, accurately described the 1971 events as the White House "horrors."

During the early years of the Nixon presidency, there was serious and lengthy discussion about using illegal means to get national security information from American citizens. On several occasions, wiretaps were placed without warrants. But the burglary of the office of Dr. Fielding constituted the most extreme and unconstitutional covert action taken to that date. Once undertaken, it was an action that could not be undone or explained away.

Why did this burglary happen? I am convinced that a collapse of integrity among those of us who conspired, ordered, and carried out this action was the principal cause. I came to this conclusion after reading dozens of accounts by others about those times and having long conversations with friends and former colleagues. We made our decisions in an emergency context. The nation faced serious foreign policy threats from the Vietnam War and the Soviet Union, while the White House staff struggled with President Nixon's penchant for secrecy, his fury at those who leaked classified documents, and his orders to investigate relentlessly those individuals he felt would compromise national security. In 1971 I firmly believed that the information we hoped to acquire from Dr. Fielding would help us prevent further leaks from undermining President Nixon's plan for ending the Vietnam War. Two and a half years later, I went to prison for approving and organizing that burglary. By then I was deeply remorseful, conflicted, and convinced that I had lost my way, in complete contrast to the ebullient good humor with which I had embarked on my great adventure in government.

Every administration brings in a huge cadre of younger staffers to fill the many crucial positions that keep the White House running. Those of us who joined the Nixon transition team to serve on John Ehrlichman's and Bob Haldeman's staffs had no experience with high government. For the most part, we were young businessmen and lawyers who had served on the 1968 campaign staff as advance men, policy analysts, speechwriters, or media experts and who had been linked professionally and personally in some way with our principals before joining the staff. Our loyalties were to our principals and to the president personally.

Long before I understood the seriousness of the many responsibilities I would be given, I was sent to New York City to work in the transition office. The Nixon transition set up shop in the Pierre Hotel in New York City, one of the most elegant and expensive hostelries in North America, and only a block away from Nixon's cooperative apartment on Fifth Avenue. He could walk to work each morning, providing numerous photo opportunities for tourists and journalists. Some of us who joined the transition staff in New York were lodged at the Wyndham Hotel, an actors' hotel located across Fifty-seventh Street from the Plaza Hotel. Like the Pierre, the Plaza was a grand place with a great tradition and astronomical prices. The most famous resident of the Wyndham during the two months I lived there was the prop dog who played in the hit musical *Annie*. Like two-legged stars, this dog had a staff of handlers who tried to keep him on leash and on schedule.

I shared an office on the eleventh floor of the Pierre with Ed Morgan, an Arizona lawyer who had also been one of John Ehrlichman's most effective advance men during the campaign. When I first met Ed, he regaled me with stories from the campaign that made me feel I had missed out on one of life's great opportunities. He was a very tall and heavyset man with a bright cherubic face. When describing the day-to-day absurdities of the campaign and local political leaders, he would explode into long riffs of increasingly off-color language that left me and anyone else within earshot helpless with laughter. He became one of my best friends over the next four years.

Ed and I were tasked to vet the stock holdings and corporate backgrounds of the president's nominees to the cabinet and sub-cabinet to make sure there were no real or apparent conflicts of interest. A federal statute prohibited an individual from holding a federal position that would enable him to benefit from that position. Not only were actual conflicts proscribed, but the appearance of conflicts was also outlawed.

One of the first sets of stocks and previous corporate responsibilities we reviewed were those of Governor John Volpe of Massachusetts. The president had nominated the governor to be secretary of Transportation. When Volpe came to meet Ed and me, we discovered that there was a clear appearance of a conflict of interest because his privately owned company, the John Volpe

Construction Company, was constructing the new Department of Transportation building in Washington, D.C. I told him that we had learned there was a big sign out in front of the construction site that said, THIS BUILDING IS BROUGHT TO YOU BY THE JOHN VOLPE CONSTRUCTION COMPANY, or words to that effect. This constituted an appearance of a conflict, and we suggested that maybe he should change the name and convey all management responsibility to someone else. He agreed to do so. The governor and his lawyer returned a few days later to report on the steps they had taken. The governor said that he had transferred all management tasks to his brother. We reviewed the document that showed his brother was directed under this shift in management to have no contact with the governor during his time of service at the Department of Transportation.

"That's great," I remember saying. "That should take care of the management issue. And what's the new name?"

"I've changed it to 'the Volpe Construction Company,'" he answered.

I looked at Ed, who was looking pensively at his desk. The mirthful twitching of his mouth indicated that he did not trust himself to respond.

I jumped in, trying my best to maintain a serious professional demeanor. "Well," I said, "we're getting closer. But I think the real problem, governor, is not the first name, but the last. Perhaps you could find a name that doesn't have 'Volpe' in it."

He agreed and told his lawyer to come up with some suggestions. After concluding our financial discussion, the governor and his lawyer got up, we all shook hands, and then they left.

Our room at the Pierre was large and had been stripped of the bed and easy chairs. Ed and I faced each other while we worked, crammed in behind two large desks. Small sitting chairs faced the sides of our desks where the cabinet nominees and their lawyers sat while we worked through their financial histories. Three doors led from the room: one that led into the hall, one into the closet, and one into the bedroom. After winding up our vetting session with one cabinet position nominee who shall remain nameless, Ed and I turned around and moved over to sit down at our desks. We sensed that the nominee turned around and, without hesitation, walked confidently into the closet, closing the door behind him. Ed and I looked at each other briefly, picked up some papers, and pretended to read through them. Had the man emerged immediately, there wouldn't have been a problem. But he delayed, excruciatingly.

Time stretched out as slowly as I can ever remember. A quick glance showed that Ed Morgan's face was becoming redder and redder. I felt my eyes begin to water, and to keep from letting any weird sounds come out, I started biting the inside of my mouth. Finally—it seemed forever—we noticed in our peripheral vision that the knob on the closet door was beginning to turn ever so slowly. Then, as we continued to look at our papers and not toward the nominee, he slowly exited through the closet door and, in his best rendition of the "Pink Panther," oozed along the wall to the other door, opened it gently, and tiptoed into the hall.

Ed Morgan exploded. He started laughing and sobbing so hard that I thought he would choke. His head dropped down onto his arms folded on his desk. My eyes were drowning in tears. I leaned back so far in my chair that I fell off on the floor, where I sat gently banging my head against the wall. The high farce completely wiped out any prospect of further work that day.

"Let's get out of here," Ed pleaded. "Twenty-seven f——ing seconds. That's how long he was in there."

To let loose our pent-up hilarity, we rushed out of the Pierre that afternoon, took a left turn, and for the next two hours walked up and down Fifth Avenue singing Broadway musical tunes. We belted out songs from *Oklahoma, The King and I, Showboat,* and whatever else came into our crazed minds. Christmas shoppers scurrying along Fifth must have concluded that we had started drinking hours earlier. We were part of the new government of the most powerful nation on earth, and it felt like the beginning of an exuberant journey on which we were all destined to ride high.

Four years later the transformation could hardly have been more complete. The laughter lasted barely into 1969, and in its place a very different mood took hold. The mood was darker, less open, more anxious, more defensive. I was never to be so happy-go-lucky in government as that afternoon at the Pierre allowed me to be.

Each of the commissions I was given during my time in the White House came with a handsomely framed certificate that included the phrase "reposing special trust in your integrity." At the time I thought nothing of the terminology; it seemed like governmental jargon, a way to make the process of taking a job more august. But in the years since, I have come back to the language of those commissions and found in it a more subtle and far-reaching moral imperative. I skipped across it as a young man; now it seems to me that integrity is one of the most important personal qualities that any individual in a position of power or responsibility can show, whether in business or politics, whether in public or private life. Trying to understand what integrity really means in those commissions has helped me develop a framework for my own life and given me a way of seeing how others in the pressure of competitive environments can avoid doing what I did. Because if you compromise your integrity, you allow a little piece of your soul to slip through your hands. Integrity, like trust, is all too easy to lose, and all too difficult to restore.

Few who knew me in 1970 would have considered me the sort of person who would break a law. Raised in a highly moral family, provided with an excellent education, including law school and the Navy, my values were those of Christian middle America. Money, outside influences, and the system itself can all be sources of the corruption that infects politics. The same can be said for elements of the business world or any other competitive environment. This book is not about individual corruption or criminality; rather, it describes the circumstances that can lead good people to make bad choices. I am no longer the person I was at twenty-nine, when I was a fresh-faced young man in government with the whole world apparently ahead of him. Sometimes I hardly recognize that younger man. It makes it easier to see his actions and decisions, for better or worse, in some kind of perspective. The young Bud Krogh wanted to do the right thing, but the correct path wasn't always clear to him. A combination of youthful naïveté, ambition, loyalty, and a military sense of duty—each a virtue in its own right and proportion—was his undoing when mixed with the rarefied elements of a career in the White House against the fever-pitch backdrop of the Vietnam War.

My friend Lynn Sutcliffe wrote the following to the judge before I was sentenced to prison in 1974:

In most situations Bud's commendable character traits would have caused him to disapprove the commission of an illegal act. The events surrounding the Fielding break-in played upon those usually commendable traits in such a way as to produce the opposite result. But to understand Bud's actions is not to excuse or condone them.

By describing the circumstances around what happened in 1971, the tumultuous events in American society at the time, and my other work in the White House, I certainly do not mean to excuse or condone my actions. I still deeply regret those actions, which worked a destructive force upon our nation. These actions and the efforts to cover them up led to a widespread distrust in our government and its leaders that continues to this day. I do, however, mean to provide a partial explanation of how somebody like myself, that is, somebody with all the advantages, somebody meaning to do well, can commit a crime—not by accident, mind you, but by skewed priorities, misplaced loyalties, overwhelming external pressures, and clouded judgment.

During my time in the White House there were many temptations and ideas that could have waylaid any of us. Ideologies, alliances, power, the ability to do good for the country and the world, all combined into a nearly intoxicating work and life environment. My story starts with a decision in the high summer of 1971, the consequences of which were quite different from what any of us had foreseen.

PART I

A Criminal Conspiracy

CHAPTER 1

Two Decisions
in Two Days

On July 15 and 17, 1971, President Richard M. Nixon made two critical national security decisions. The first decision will go down in the history books as one of the boldest acts of diplomacy in the twentieth century. The second decision, which embroiled me in more personal difficulties than I could ever have imagined, led to the downfall of the Nixon presidency.

On the evening of the first day, July 15, the president told the world that on July 11, Dr. Henry Kissinger had conducted secret talks with Premier Chou En-Lai of China, during which Chou invited Nixon to visit China "before May 1972." The president said that he had accepted Chou's invitation with pleasure. His subsequent visit to China in February 1972, hinted at in his writings and numerous comments over the previous four years, constituted the most dramatic and, to knowledgeable experts in U.S. foreign policy, the most significant achievement of the Nixon presidency.

I had been at an impromptu visit by Nixon to the Lincoln Memorial at 4:45 A.M. on May 9, 1970, a few days after he had decided to invade Cambodia. During an hourlong discussion with a group of stunned students who had come to protest his actions, he told them that he had "great hopes that during my administration . . . the great mainland of China would be opened up so that we could know the 700 million people who live in China, who are one of the most remarkable people on earth." That foreshadowing of his intention to open China finally climaxed with his electrifying announcement to the world on July 15, 1971.

The morning of July 17, the president presided over a meeting that I attended on the patio outside his office at the western White House in San Clemente, California. The western White House included the president's home, "La Casa Pacifica," an ornate white stucco and red-tiled building located just to the north of a small, one-story office building complex that contained offices for the president, senior staff, and the traveling White House entourage. La Casa Pacifica was a beautiful Spanish-style mansion with a magnificent view, perched on the bluffs above the best surfing beach in southern California. The president purchased it in 1969, and it had become his residence when he took extended vacations away from Washington, D.C.

The view from the patio outside the president's office was also spectacular, and we could see a U.S. Navy destroyer steaming through the whitecaps just off the coast in the bright morning sunshine, providing security for the president and his family. The Casa Pacifica office complex was located just to the north of the Camp Pendleton Marine Corps base. With the Marines to the south, the Navy to the west, and the Secret Service embedded in various posts around the western White House, the president lived and worked in a sort of militarized high-security resort.

The purpose of the July 17 meeting was to report to the president on the progress of a major administration effort he had launched a few weeks before to curb the use of heroin by our soldiers in Vietnam. Except for the president and John Ehrlichman, the other meeting attendees—Dr. Jerome Jaffe, Dr. Benny Primm, and I—were jet-lagged from our respective trips. We sat around a glass patio table, enjoying the sunshine as we presented the president with a thorough report on our findings. The president looked tanned and rested, and his mood was ebullient, the result of the overwhelmingly positive response to his China announcement two nights before.

I had just returned the day before from two weeks of travel to France, Greece, Turkey, India, Thailand, Laos, and Vietnam; I had been assessing the effectiveness of our international narcotics control programs in these countries. The results had been mixed so far, with good results in curbing the growth of poppies in Turkey but less success in preventing the flow of heroin into South Vietnam. During my trip I had met with action officers in the State Department, the CIA, the Bureau of Narcotics and Dangerous Drugs, the Bureau of Customs, and the U.S. Military Command in Vietnam, telling all of them about the president's strong commitment to reducing the flow of illegal drugs into the United States.

My final foreign stop on the two-week trip was in South Vietnam, where I joined up with Dr. Jaffe, the newly designated chief of the Special Action Office for Drug Abuse Prevention; Seth Rosenberg, Dr. Jaffe's assistant; and Dr. Primm, one of Jaffe's principal drug treatment advisers. They met me in South Vietnam so that we could take a firsthand look at the urinalysis centers the military had recently set up at the president's direction in Long Binh and Cam Ranh Bay. The machines in these centers tested for the presence of opiates in a soldier's urine. If he tested positive, a soldier would need to go through treatment before being released into civilian life. Long Binh and Cam Ranh Bay were the principal debarkation centers for U.S. soldiers leaving

Vietnam following their tours of duty. The handmade sign above the entrance to the center at Long Binh proclaimed its purpose: THE PEE HOUSE OF THE AUGUST MOON.

During our stop in South Vietnam we also had visited several military facilities, met with commanders and their staffs, and observed the functioning of the diagnostic system. In our meetings we became acutely aware of the toll the war was taking on our soldiers, and we promised to provide all the help we could. We were encouraged to learn that the diagnostic system we had just instituted showed lower numbers of opiate use by our soldiers than we had expected. In our meeting with the president, we reported the findings that the number of U.S. military personnel who tested positive for opiates in their systems, approximately 4.5 percent, was well below the 20 percent figure that had been reported in the press. The president told us how pleased he was with the results so far and encouraged us to move ahead aggressively with the program. He said that he was glad that the percentages showed that 96 percent of those who came back from Vietnam could be employed and move back into society without fear of being drug users. Following this meeting with the president, Dr. Jaffe, Dr. Primm, and I briefed the television pool reporters on the meeting and the results of the trip.

What gave me the most satisfaction that day was the conviction that our Vietnam drug program would help us alleviate the perception among some Americans, especially business leaders, that the Vietnam veteran was a ruthless killer, a junkie, and therefore unemployable. The president was committed to changing this image. He had told me and others in a previous meeting on June 3, 1971, that narcotics would be an issue used by adversaries to his Vietnam policy to impugn the military, so it was both a political issue and a real issue. With the lower number of positive tests among our soldiers than what we had anticipated, I felt we had made a solid contribution to defending against any opposition to the president's Vietnam policy based on the narcotics issue. Following lunch at the western White House with Dr. Jaffe, I was feeling very good about what we had accomplished and was looking forward to some rest and relaxation before returning to Washington, D.C. But this was not to be. John Ehrlichman's secretary found me and said that he wanted to see me as soon as it was convenient. This always meant immediately.

When I was waved into John Ehrlichman's office, he got up and quietly closed the door behind me. This surprised me because his office was already in the innermost sanctum of offices closest to the president's own. Any additional secrecy afforded by a closed door didn't seem necessary to me at the time. Then he told me about the president's second national security decision.

I sat down in a chair in front of his desk, and he handed me a bulky file labeled "Pentagon Papers." I leafed through the contents, which included newspaper reprints of the Pentagon Papers, news stories about the papers and about the Supreme Court's rejection of the government's request to restrain their publication, and various internal memos. As I read, Ehrlichman told me that the assignment he was about to give me had been deemed of the highest national security importance by the president. He emphasized that the president was as angry about the leak of the Pentagon Papers as he had ever seen him on any other issue.

In his dry style, Ehrlichman said that while I had been junketing around the world working on drug programs and policies, he, Bob Haldeman, Henry Kissinger, and Chuck Colson had been working hard and meeting regularly with the president to determine how best to respond to the leak of the Pentagon Papers, which he described as a "crisis." According to Ehrlichman, the president was certain that a conspiracy was involved in the release of the Pentagon Papers and that we needed to run our own investigation to find out who was part of the conspiracy. He said that the president didn't believe that a thorough investigation could be carried out by the FBI or the Department of Justice (DOJ). Consequently, he had ordered that an independent White House team be set up to begin its own investigation immediately. This new team would investigate the ramifications of the release of the Pentagon Papers to the press by Daniel Ellsberg, a former Pentagon military analyst. The investigation was to have the highest priority, and preparations were to begin that day.

Ehrlichman told me that a decision had also been made to share responsibility for the Pentagon Papers investigation between a representative from Kissinger's National Security Council staff and one from Ehrlichman's Domestic Council staff. Ehrlichman had assigned me to be a codirector of the investigation, and Kissinger had assigned David Young, one of his closest personal aides, to be the other codirector. All personal and written reports were to go to Ehrlichman, who was to be the channel to the president. He told me that Chuck Colson, a special counsel to the president, would assign someone from his group to work with us as well.

It was a lot to digest in one short meeting. The idea of making a team—soon to be known as the Special Investigations Unit (SIU)—out of three people drawn from three different staffs, each person with primary loyalty to his own boss, seemed to me to be at best unwieldy, if not impossible to manage effectively. I did not express any misgivings to Ehrlichman at the time, however, since I felt that this was the most critical assignment I had yet been given on Nixon's staff and it was not for me to question the wisdom of the structure.

Nixon's White House staff comprised several individual fiefdoms. Staff members had been hired on the basis of loyalty to the president and to the senior presidential aide who had recruited him or her. This created independent chains of loyalty—

effectively clans—all the way up to the president. While there was regular communication and cooperation—and endless meetings—among the staffs, there was no doubt about the senior staff person to whom a junior staff member owed primary allegiance. This resulted in a less cohesive and monolithic White House than most people imagined.

In my case, I felt deep loyalty to John Ehrlichman. My being in the White House was in part based on fifteen years of friendship between the Ehrlichman and Krogh families. The unquestioning zeal with which I approached the Pentagon Papers assignment—unquestioning not only about our mission but also about my ability to carry out the work—was rooted in the depth of the connection I had with John Ehrlichman.

When my parents passed away in 1962, John Ehrlichman became a surrogate father to me. Both Ehrlichman and Richard Nixon would be strong male role models to me, and after my father's death when I was twenty-two, I was increasingly dependent on strong male role models for guidance. My father had been a giant in my life—a man of great accomplishment, wisdom, and grace. He died during the third month of my four-month Navy officer candidate school (OCS) program. I had to make a decision during the weekend of his passing: whether to take emergency leave and go home for a period of time or stay with my company, where I was serving as assistant company commander, maintain the integrity of that command structure until we were commissioned, and complete my training. I asked myself what my dad would have wanted, and it was clear that he would have told me to finish the job at hand.

While I was in the Navy, John Ehrlichman and I stayed in close touch, and he helped me get accepted to the University of Washington Law School in 1968. From the first year of law school, I aspired to work in his Seattle law firm upon graduation.

During law school I clerked for his law firm and concentrated my law studies and articles on land use and environmental law, the two areas in which Ehrlichman specialized.

The relationship on the family side was very close. My wife Suzanne and I enjoyed many events with the Ehrlichman family: Christmas Eve parties, Thanksgiving Day touch football games, salmon bakes, and skiing trips. We even babysat for the five Ehrlichman children during an extended trip that John and his wife Jeanne took.

John Ehrlichman's brilliance, command of the English language, and sense of humor were well known in Seattle and were on display as soon as he joined the White House staff. His early White House press briefing in which he described getting lost on a family vacation while navigating the maze of parkways across the Potomac between the Iwo Jima monument, the Pentagon, and Memorial Bridge was talked about for years in the press room. He had a sharp wit and a strong sense of the sardonic. Two phrases he coined, "It'll play in Peoria" and "Let him twist slowly, slowly in the wind," entered the American political lexicon as soon as they were uttered.

One evening in Washington Suzanne and I were invited to join the Ehrlichman family for a performance of *Godspell* at the Ford Theater. Spotting Alice Roosevelt Longworth, the eighty-two-year-old daughter of President Teddy Roosevelt and uncontested doyenne of Washington society, he got up and took me over to meet her. He had met her before, and after a pleasant greeting he said, "I'd like Bud Krogh to meet you, Mrs. Longworth." "How do you do," she said. "And what do you do for Mr. Ehrlichman?" Before I could answer, Ehrlichman said, "He serves as my Bob Cratchit."

Ehrlichman had an incredible memory. He once dazzled the Washington State Supreme Court when he brilliantly argued a complex land use case on the morning after Richard Nixon's plane had landed in Seattle for an overnight campaign stop. For the previous three months, Ehrlichman had been serving the Nixon campaign as tour director, and he had had no opportunity to review the briefs and documents during that time. The only preparation time he had was in the car with me as I drove him to Olympia, Washington, where he would argue the case. During his oral argument to the court, he was in total command of all the relevant facts, the issues, and the points of law in the case. As the junior associate on the case, I was simply awed by his performance. We found out later—a short time after we were working in the West Wing of the White House—that he had won the case by a close vote of five to four. I felt that it was Ehrlichman's brilliant advocacy that won the day.

Right after Nixon won the 1968 election on November 5, Ehrlichman met with the president-elect and senior campaign staff in California to determine how the transition office and the new White House would be staffed. The president-elect asked Ehrlichman to serve as counsel to the president. A few days later Ehrlichman returned to Seattle to shut down his law practice and prepare for his move to the East Coast. The first day after his return from California, he came into my office, sat back in his chair, and put his feet up on my desk. "Do you like your work here?" he asked me with a mischievous smile.

"Yes, sir, I do," I answered.

"Would you consider changing it and coming to Washington, D.C., to serve as staff assistant to the counsel to the president?" he asked, raising his left eyebrow as he said it.

My answer was immediate. "Yes, sir, I certainly would!" I felt overwhelmed and elated at the opportunity that he was giving me.

While he was intensely competitive and hated to lose in lawsuits or in games, he also possessed a great heart and could be counted on to help family and friends when the chips were down. Years later, when I told him about my impending divorce, he burst into tears of sympathy.

This was the John Ehrlichman who took me aside in San Clemente: a family friend, a father figure, a brilliant mentor, an employer, and the principal person to whom I owed complete personal loyalty on the Nixon staff. As we finished our meeting that afternoon on July 16 in San Clemente, Ehrlichman said that the president had expressly ordered that before starting any work on this assignment I was to read the chapter on the Hiss case in his book *Six Crises*. Ehrlichman stressed that it was important to infer from *Six Crises* what the president thought was at stake with Ellsberg's release of the Pentagon Papers and how the investigation should be approached.

That evening of July 17, I went back to my room in the Newporter Inn, twenty miles north of the western White House. A number of White House staff members were staying at the Newporter while the president was in residence in San Clemente. I ordered dinner and sat down to read.

A few years earlier I had read *Six Crises* to get a better understanding of Nixon because Ehrlichman had worked for him as an advance man in the 1960 presidential campaign and later as tour director for Nixon's 1962 campaign for governor of California. While visiting Ehrlichman at the 1962 campaign headquarters on Wilshire Boulevard in Los Angeles, I was captivated by the mechanics of running a campaign and wished I could participate. But as a recently commissioned naval officer stationed on the USS *Yorktown*, an antisubmarine warfare aircraft carrier, I wasn't in a position in June 1962 to offer my services to the campaign.

When I first read *Six Crises* soon after its publication, I had been impressed not only with the way Nixon had worked through some extremely demanding challenges but also with the quality of his writing. But this time it read differently: now it was an assignment from the author—as president—to delve into one chapter, to glean the substantive ideas, and to learn how he wanted us to approach a major national security investigation. Why did Nixon direct me to read the chapter on Hiss before starting the investigation? First, I think Nixon wanted me to understand unequivocally that he viewed the problems with Ellsberg's release of the Pentagon Papers as a full national security crisis, one comparable to the career-defining—for him—conviction of a traitor in the full glare of publicity in 1948. Nixon was offering me the chance to succeed as he had succeeded and to draw the obvious inference about what such a success might portend for my own future career in government. Nixon was sure that Ellsberg had not functioned alone and that there were other conspirators who must have helped to get the Pentagon Papers out into the public arena. The president felt that their purpose was clearly to undermine his policies for ending the Vietnam War. (Much later, in 2004, Daniel Ellsberg confirmed to me that if he had had access to Nixon's current Vietnam War plans in 1971, he would certainly have released them to the press. He felt that Nixon was more committed to winning the Vietnam War than ending it.)

As I read the Hiss chapter, I tried hard to understand who Hiss really was and his relevance to the Ellsberg case. Alger Hiss was a high-ranking official in the State Department who had participated in some of the most significant foreign policy events of the 1940s. He was present at Yalta with Roosevelt, Churchill, and Stalin. He was a well-established and respected member of the foreign policy elite, with impeccable academic credentials. And he was a traitor.

I learned about the key role played by Whittaker Chambers in uncovering the truth about Hiss. Chambers, a self-professed former Communist, disclosed under oath to the House Un-American Activities Committee (HUAC) that he knew Hiss well because they were both members of a Soviet spy ring operating in the United States. When Hiss was questioned under oath about whether he knew Chambers, he said he didn't know a man with the name of Whittaker Chambers. He was emphatic before Congress and elsewhere that he didn't know Chambers. After a period of intense questioning by the committee between August and December 1948, it was clear that Hiss was lying. Eventually convicted of perjury by the Department of Justice, he served a forty-four-month prison sentence. Nixon, by his own account in *Six Crises*, worked relentlessly on the case and frequently put in eighteen-hour days to put Hiss away.

The first and most basic impression I got from reading the Hiss chapter was that Nixon viewed the uncovering of the truth about Hiss as vital to the national security. He wrote on page 10 of *Six Crises* that the House Committee on Un-American Activities, on which he served, "had an obligation running to the very security of the nation to dig out the truth." On page 40 he added: "But this case involved far more than the personal fortunes of Hiss, Chambers, myself, or the members of the Committee. *It involved the security of the whole nation and the cause of free men everywhere*" (emphasis added). It was a heroic endeavor, evidently, deeply connected to preserving American freedoms. What cause could be nobler? In reading the stirring sentences that emphasized Nixon's view that solving the Hiss case was a vital national security interest, I realized that he saw a parallel in Ellsberg's leak of the Pentagon Papers, but I overlooked one point: in both cases there was no doubt in Nixon's mind that the man in question was a traitor, long before there was any actual proof.

Although I did not recall it that evening, the year before, on August 3, 1970, President Nixon had publicly proclaimed guilt in a case before actual evidence was presented. When Charles Manson went to trial, Nixon had told the press right at the start that here was a man "who was guilty, directly or indirectly, of eight murders without reason." Because Manson was on trial and not convicted, the president's statement was fiercely criticized. Outrage came from many quarters condemning the president for asserting guilt before trial in a country where a person is presumed innocent until proven guilty.

I learned about Nixon's comment later that same day at the beginning of a major meeting I was running in Denver for the president and law enforcement officials from all fifty states. The purpose of the meeting was to emphasize the administration's new major financial support for state and local law enforcement. Ron Ziegler, the White House press secretary, came up to me before I opened the session and whispered, "It doesn't matter what you do in this meeting. No one will know. The president just told the world that Manson is guilty. We're going to be putting this fire out for the next few hours." I was deeply disappointed because of the time and effort so many people had put into the plan, advance, and management of the meeting. While returning to Washington, D.C., on Air Force One with the president, Ehrlichman, Ziegler, and I drafted a White House press release explaining that the president did not mean to assert guilt, but that he was referring to allegations and that the presumption of innocence was bedrock law in our country. We hadn't finished the press release by the time the plane was approaching Andrews Air Force Base, so we delayed landing, boring circular holes in the sky, until we finally had a release acceptable to the staff and the president. After Air Force One landed, the press plane touched down, and we handed the release out to the press as they trooped off.

While reading *Six Crises* that evening, I did not discern the propensity of the president to rush to judgment without proof in the Manson case and his judgment before trial that Ellsberg was a traitor. I simply accepted the president's opinion.

On page 67 of *Six Crises*, Nixon wrote:

> As Herbert Hoover wrote me after Hiss' conviction, "at last the stream of treason that has existed in our government has been exposed in a fashion all may believe.". . . . The Hiss case aroused the nation for the first time to the existence and character of the Communist conspiracy within the United States.

The real meaning that I was supposed to derive from reading the chapter on Hiss was that Hiss had conspirators in the spy ring, that it really was a national security crisis, and that Nixon had pulled out all the stops to put an end to Hiss's career as a spy. It was clear that Nixon hoped I would use a no less aggressive and intense approach in pursuit of Ellsberg, who to Nixon was clearly a traitor on the scale of Hiss and no doubt working with others to undermine the security of the United States. I finished reading the Hiss chapter very late that night. The next day, July 18, I reread some of the pertinent sections, reviewed the contents of the bucket file that Ehrlichman had given me, and, with the president and staff, returned to Washington on Air Force One.

After reading the chapter and absorbing the lessons, I felt overwhelmed by the expectation that was being placed on me. I knew I had to commit a huge amount of time to establishing a new organization to direct the international narcotics control program, and I didn't know where I would find the time to do the Pentagon Papers job correctly. Someone with fewer other direct responsibilities would have to run day-to-day operations. We also needed help from an experienced investigator. As I prepared for the new work, I read that the Pentagon Papers described the errors in the Vietnam and Indochina policies of presidents before

Nixon took office in 1968. Nothing in the papers related to Nixon's policies. But I didn't question the reasons why Nixon was so driven to investigate Ellsberg.

In reflecting from the vantage point of today on what the president really wanted from the investigation and why I was given the assignment, I have been able to gain a great deal of insight from the transcripts of taped conversations in two other meetings in the Oval Office two weeks before my fateful meeting with Ehrlichman on July 17.

Both meetings were held on July 1, 1971, the first from 8:45 A.M. to 9:52 A.M. with the president, Bob Haldeman, and Henry Kissinger in attendance, and the second from 10:28 A.M. to 11:49 A.M. with the president, Bob Haldeman, Chuck Colson, and John Ehrlichman. Both meetings were tape-recorded and have been reprinted in *The New Nixon Tapes: Abuse of Power*.

In the first meeting, during discussions about the Pentagon Papers, the president said, "This is what I want. I have a project that I want somebody to take it just like I took the Hiss case. . . . And I'll tell you what. This takes—this takes eighteen hours a day. It takes devotion and dedication and loyalty and diligence such as you've never seen, Bob. I've never worked as hard in my life, and I'll never work as hard again because I don't have the energy for it. But this thing is a hell of a great opportunity because here is what it is."

In the second meeting that morning, the president discussed with Haldeman, Colson, and Ehrlichman the Supreme Court's June 30, 1971, ruling against the government. The administration had attempted to prevent the *New York Times* from publishing the Pentagon Papers and had been rebuffed. Nixon's bitterness about the decision was obvious. In the transcript of that meeting, Nixon said, "We're through with this sort of court case. . . . Go back and read the chapter on the Hiss case in *Six*

Crises and you'll see how it was done. It wasn't done waiting for the goddamn courts or the attorney general or the FBI. . . . We have got to get going here."

In the most relevant section, which relates directly to their decision to pick me for the job, the president said:

> Now do you see what we need? I really need a son of a bitch . . . who will work his butt off and do it dishonorably. Do you see what I mean? Who will know what he's doing and I want to know too. And I'll direct him myself. I know how to play this game, and we're going to start playing it.
>
> I can't have a high-minded lawyer like John Ehrlichman, or, you know, Dean or somebody like that. I want somebody just as tough as I am for a change. These kids don't understand, they have no understanding of politics, no understanding of public relations. John Mitchell is that way, John is always worried about is it technically correct. Do you think, for chrissake, that the *New York Times* is worried about all the legal niceties? Those sons of bitches are killing me. I mean, thank God I leaked to the press during the Hiss controversy. This is what we've got to get. I want you to shake these [unintelligible] up around here. Now you do it. Shake them up. Get them off their goddamn dead asses, we're up against an enemy, a conspiracy. They're using any means. We are going to use any means. Is that clear?
>
> Did they get the Brookings Institution raided last night? No? Get it done. I want it done. I want the Brookings Institution's safe cleaned out, and have it cleaned out in a way that it makes somebody else [responsible].

So why did I get the assignment? I speculate that I can hardly have been the first choice. Nixon had wanted a black ops (operations) kind of guy, a "real son of a bitch." While I can't confirm the president's exact feelings about my character at the time, I don't think he viewed me as a "real son of a bitch." At the time my ironic nickname from colleagues was "Evil" Krogh; I had a reputation as a somewhat rigid moral do-gooder. Others were more obvious candidates to run the investigation, none more so than Chuck Colson. I have always been curious as to why Colson wasn't given the principal responsibility for the Special Investigations Unit. He came to the White House with a reputation as a can-do kind of guy. He was willing to play political hardball. He even had a cartoon on his office wall showing a Vietnamese peasant with somebody's hand holding his testicles. Caption: "When you've got 'em by the balls their hearts and minds will follow."

So why wasn't Colson given the assignment of heading up the SIU? It may have been that Ehrlichman and Haldeman were afraid of Colson. They were concerned that because Colson had a direct line to the president and was known to appeal to Nixon's darker side of paranoia and anger—his dark angels—he would do things that would be dangerous and risky to the White House and the president. It was, of course, ironic that I—"Evil" Krogh—would conduct dangerous and risky activities, despite a dearth of direct experience in black bag operations or direct access to the president and his dark side.

Another possible candidate for the Pentagon Papers job was John Dean, counsel to the president. But I learned much later that Dean—to his great credit—had single-handedly prevented the Brookings Institution raid from going forward as the president had expressly ordered on July 1, 1971. When Dean learned about the planned raid, he immediately flew to California and persuaded Ehrlichman to call it off. As a result of this courageous act, Dean was then viewed by Ehrlichman, Colson, and Haldeman as not aggressive enough to carry out the president's wishes.

Dean told me later that the reason he was not selected for the SIU was that he was viewed as a "little old lady" by the senior staff. We all would have been better off with Dean's "little old lady" perspective.

I learned much later, too, that Pat Buchanan, one of the president's favorite speechwriters, had turned down the assignment. He felt that it was more of an operational responsibility than a task for a White House policymaker and writer.

I guess I was chosen because I was the White House liaison with the FBI and the Department of Justice. I was often assigned to resolve challenging problems for the administration such as crime in the District of Columbia, our responses to antiwar protests, and the narcotics control programs. I was interested in the operational aspects of problem-solving. Even though I don't think I fit the dark profile the president wanted for the job, perhaps a simpler reason I got it was that it was understood that I would take it, do it to the best of my ability, and not ask questions. At that point in my White House career, I wasn't given to lengthy reflection on whether I was competent or experienced enough to do the jobs assigned to me. I certainly wasn't in the habit of questioning the orders or wisdom of my superiors, John Ehrlichman and Richard Nixon, to whom I gave complete loyalty. I suppose that I fit the other criterion the president spoke of on July 1: I was diligent, dedicated, and devoted to him.

So I accepted the task, and despite my other responsibilities, I set about making the time to manage a team that would have the highest priority to solve what I believed was a real national security problem. The Special Investigations Unit was a unit in name only. My first priority was to equip it with a discreet base. Then I had to find the plumbers.

CHAPTER 2

The Plumbers
Gather in Room 16

On July 19, the day after my return to Washington, D.C., I debriefed members of my staff on my trip around the world on narcotics control issues. In addition to the follow-up work for the military drug program in South Vietnam, we had been directed by the president to move forward aggressively on forming the Cabinet Committee for International Narcotics Control. By bringing together the lead agencies with foreign responsibilities under the chairmanship of the secretary of State, William Rogers, we felt that we would have an effective organization to design and implement strong drug interdiction policies around the world. I was designated to serve as Secretary Rogers's executive director of the cabinet committee. Turning to the special investigations work right after these briefings, I called G. Gordon Liddy and set up an appointment with him for the following day. Because of his previous experience as an FBI agent, prosecutor, and Republican loyalist, Liddy had received an appointment as special assistant to the secretary in the Treasury Department's law enforcement section. Gerald Ford, GOP minority leader in the House, had helped Liddy join the administration in March 1969, six weeks after President Nixon's inauguration.

Liddy had worked with me on numerous projects dealing with the narcotics interdiction programs under the Customs Service and gun control issues under the Bureau of Alcohol, Tobacco, and Firearms (ATF). A passionate gun enthusiast and loyal member of the National Rifle Association (NRA), Liddy argued aggressively and effectively in policy discussions against some of the more restrictive gun control initiatives that circulated in the administration. After he joined the SIU, I learned that during one of his legal arguments in a crowded courtroom Liddy had discharged a pistol to make a point. This apparently scared the wits out of those present and incurred a quick censure from the judge.

Liddy was also a friend of one of my best friends in the Justice Department, Donald Santarelli, who was serving as the associate deputy attorney general for policy. Santarelli, like Liddy, held strong conservative views, and both men advocated for muscular law enforcement tactics in the president's wars on crime and drugs. Santarelli had told me on several occasions how difficult a time Liddy was having at Treasury because of his numerous run-ins and conflicts with Eugene Rossides, the assistant secretary of the Treasury for law enforcement. He suggested that if it were possible to find another position for Liddy in the administration, this move would be good for Liddy as well as for the policies we wanted to push forward.

Attorney General John Mitchell agreed with Santarelli that it would be a good move if Liddy could be brought to the White House. In a memo dated June 15, 1971, Santarelli confirmed that the attorney general was committed to finding a spot for Liddy on the White House staff. In an assignment that would surprise no one today, his areas of concentration would be narcotics and guns.

To do my job well, I felt it was critical to maintain a good professional and personal relationship with Attorney General Mitchell. In late November 1968, during the transition period from President Johnson to President-Elect Nixon, I had my first meeting with Mitchell at Nixon, Mudge, Rose, Guthrie & Alexander. This was the law firm where Mitchell and Nixon had worked as partners and where Mitchell had presided as Nixon's manager for the 1968 campaign. Mitchell was brusque, laconic, and somewhat sour when we first met, and he kept puffing on his pipe while we discussed several issues. But we became friends and stayed friendly over the next two years.

In July 1971, Mitchell had close and easy access to the president. So as the president's liaison with the Justice Department, I wanted to stay in Mitchell's good graces as much as I could. Hiring Liddy would help on all fronts.

On several occasions when I called Mitchell in the evening, I ended up talking with his wife, Martha, a loquacious southern belle who had long blond hair and a vivacious smile and who tried to look younger than her years. She was also known for her uninhibited social behavior and inability to keep her personal views about the president and administration members to herself. Even though she became known as "the voice that launched a thousand quips," Mitchell adored her. At one of the first inaugural balls in 1969, I had found myself standing next to Mitchell. Martha was dancing with wild abandon with one of the ubiquitous military aides. Mitchell followed her every move like a cat. "Isn't she beautiful?" he said to me. "Absolutely beautiful, Mr. Mitchell. Really, really stunning!" I replied.

As a result of Santarelli's and Mitchell's efforts and my own need for another staff person who could help with my narcotics and law enforcement responsibilities, Liddy officially joined the White House staff on July 20, 1971. All of the paperwork had been done and the transfer from Treasury had been completed when he came over to my office, room 172 in the Old Executive Office Building (known to everyone as "the EOB").

Room 172 and a set of suites across the hall, plus a few more offices down the center hall of the second floor of the EOB, were allocated to me and my staff when I was promoted to deputy assistant to the president for domestic affairs in early 1970. My office was painted yellow and had a very high ceiling, deep plush dark blue carpeting, and elegant furniture in the Williamsburg style. Through the windows and from my porch, there was an extraordinary view of the White House and the north lawn where reporters then and today give their nightly news reports. It was located three offices north of Nixon's hideaway office, which he frequently occupied when he needed to get away from the constant interactions in the West Wing and the Oval Office.

Office location in the Nixon White House reflected in large part the status of the staff member and was controlled with Prussian precision by Bob Haldeman, the chief of staff. The most senior positions—the chief of staff, the national security adviser, the head of congressional relations, various cabinet-level counselors to the president, and their immediate staffs—all had offices in the West Wing.

My first job on the staff had been staff assistant to the counsel to the president. John Ehrlichman was counsel to the president, so my office was a tiny office across from his much larger, wood-paneled office on the second floor of the West Wing. To help compensate for my lack of experience, Jana Hruska, John Ehrlichman's secretary and daughter of Nebraska senator Roman Hruska, took on the job of educating me in the ways of Washington. She knew everyone of importance in the Capitol and kept me from making bonehead blunders in protocol and professional courtesies. "Yes, Bud," she would admonish, "you *do* call a senator back within an hour of his call. A congressman can wait a couple of hours. You must always take a cabinet secretary's call immediately. And your wife's!"

Ehrlichman's office was directly above the Oval Office. Quite frequently when I was in his office, he would get buzzed on his phone from the line that was identified as "POTUS," for "President of the United States." Ehrlichman would pick up the phone, hit the POTUS button, and discuss some matter briefly, often with a "Yes, Mr. President," or, "No, Mr. President." If he said, "Yes, sir, I'll be right there," he'd hang up and say something like, "Okay, down the flag pole to the leader of the Western world," and rush out the door.

I sized up my new staff member when Liddy walked into room 172, my office in the EOB. He was about five-foot-ten, two inches shorter than me, and carried himself with ramrod-erect posture. A dark-complexioned man, he had thinning brown hair and heavy eyebrows over piercing dark eyes. He sported a bushy mustache and moved with a forceful, purposeful energy. When we shook hands, his grip was vise-like.

I formally welcomed him to the White House and my staff and expressed some regret that I had been unable to get him on board sooner. However, when Rossides and his colleague at the Treasury Department, Charles Walker, the deputy secretary, had heard about Liddy's transfer to the White House, they were extremely angry. They told me that they feared Liddy would undermine their policy advice to the president on gun control issues and insisted that Liddy have no policy responsibility for gun control policy while serving on my staff. Their position was way beyond their prerogative once he worked for me. We worked out a way for Liddy to continue to work on gun control matters by advising Geoffrey Shepard, another staff member of mine, who had direct responsibility for gun control policy.

Liddy said that he understood how difficult it had been to get the transfer done but was just glad to be there. Liddy was the kind of guy you'd want next to you in a foxhole, where he'd cover your back and take a bullet to save your life. He projected a warrior-type charisma and seemed to possess a great deal of physical courage. He was tough, smart, disciplined, and loyal. In the following years during the Watergate investigations, Liddy never "squealed" or "snitched" on anyone.

But there was also a strain of fanaticism in Liddy's character that I did not fully appreciate in the early weeks of our work together. His silence and conviction to stay true to his personal code of honor long after others had sold out prompted me once to liken him to Lieutenant Hiroo Onoda, the Japanese officer who refused to surrender and fought his own personal war in the Philippines for twenty-nine years after the surrender by the Japanese empire in 1945.

I told Liddy that since we had first started talking about his joining my staff to work on narcotics, bombing, and guns, another project had come up. This project, which was related directly to national security, was of utmost gravity and importance to the president. I told him that it would require all of his background and skill as a former FBI special agent and would involve the most intense effort over the next several weeks. He told me that he was there to serve the president, and me, in any way he could and that he would be honored to take on a critical national security project.

With his consent to work on the project, I took Liddy over to meet David Young. Young had already been assigned to the Special Investigations Unit from Henry Kissinger's staff while I was in San Clemente. Because there was so much urgency to get under way, Young had arranged to use a temporary office near mine until another secure office location could be found elsewhere in the EOB.

When I brought Liddy in to meet Young, Young stood up and shook Liddy's hand. While I knew both men were accomplished lawyers and had graduated from excellent law schools—Young from Cornell and Liddy from Fordham—I could immediately see some stark differences between them in personal appearance and mannerisms. Where Liddy was dark, forceful, and packed with intense emotional energy, Young was light-complexioned, laid-back, and somewhat professorial in his demeanor. With thinning blond hair and light blue eyes set in a narrow face, Young smiled a lot and spoke in whispered tones. He looked like a quintessential Englishman, the kind of man depicted in World War II films who flew fighters for the Royal Air Force during the 1940 blitz bombing of London and who would always understate the dangers he faced. I felt that the skills of each man as I knew them would be used to the maximum over the weeks ahead.

We talked briefly about the nature of the project—to investigate all aspects of the Pentagon Papers release to the press—but we did not get into any depth that first day. We did discuss the reporting arrangements. Although Young came from Henry Kissinger's staff, all information developed by the unit would be routed to John Ehrlichman, not to Kissinger. This reporting arrangement had been established by Ehrlichman in San Clemente. As far as I was aware, Kissinger was not informed by Young about any of the investigative work of the Plumbers. Ehrlichman was responsible for what was communicated to the president. I told them that I had not been instructed personally by the president but had received all of my direction from Ehrlichman in San Clemente. I told them that I had not been relieved of my primary duties on narcotics control, and in particular that I would be extremely busy over the next few weeks in setting up the Cabinet Committee for International Narcotics Control.

Young confirmed that he would be working with the unit full-time and that, as the on-site codirector of the unit, he would have primary responsibility for the day-to-day, even hour-by-hour, flow of information by memo and phone call. Young also said that he would take the responsibility for drafting the memos generated by the unit unless Liddy was given a specific written assignment. Liddy was asked later to prepare a memorandum on the less-than-satisfactory support and backup of the FBI during the subsequent work of the unit. His memorandum received wide circulation in the White House, up to and including the president.

Liddy accepted this administrative setup, which required him to take direction from both Young and myself on the work of the Special Investigations Unit. I also made it clear that on any other assignment related to narcotics or gun control Liddy worked for me.

Now it was time to find a secure home for the SIU. Room 16 was located at the farthest southwest corner on the first floor of the EOB. When I first explored the former mail room area where room 16 would be located, I thought it would be too exposed for the kind of ultra-sensitive, secret work we would be doing. In fact, the space proved secure partly because by its very ordinariness it managed to hide itself in plain sight. Staff members and support people who worked in offices along the south and west corridors of the EOB would frequently walk right by room 16. Heavy bars covered the thick glass in the windows that looked out on Seventeenth Street to the west and to the adjacent park and the Ellipse to the south. Only the designation ROOM 16 was visible on the high, nondescript, dark-paneled door. Even though there was some exposure to regular foot traffic, it was still apart from the regularly traveled corridors, and so I was able to get from my main office to room 16 quickly and without drawing much attention to where I was going. It took about three days to get the space up and running.

Toward the end of our first week, E. Howard Hunt came to the unit and introduced himself to me and David Young. He said that Chuck Colson had assigned him to work with the unit and that Colson would be interested in any information uncovered by the unit during its investigation of Ellsberg. Ehrlichman told me that Hunt, not I, would be the channel to Colson for this information. Colson was to be in charge of communicating information to the media and Congress.

A short, dapper man, Hunt had a sharp, aquiline nose, light features, sandy hair, and a ready smile. He told us that he had had a long career with the CIA, had run agents primarily in Latin America, and had been involved in the Bay of Pigs invasion in 1961. My reaction to this was to want to know a whole lot more about his involvement. The Bay of Pigs had, after all, been nothing short of a foreign policy disaster for the Kennedy administration. I learned later that Hunt believed that President Kennedy had made some bad decisions in the Bay of Pigs crisis that resulted in the deaths of many of his former colleagues in the anti-Castro Cuban community. He said that while he was not officially working for "the Agency" any longer, he had maintained good contacts there who could be useful to us.

During this first meeting with Hunt, I was struck by how unassuming, retiring, and diffident he seemed. He could blend easily into any group without drawing undue attention to himself, a valuable characteristic for a spy.

Hunt felt that it would be helpful for him to have a special secure phone for his personal use. Kathy Chenow, the secretary brought to work for the unit, set up this phone with all bills to be sent to her home address. In addition to Hunt's special phone, a "scrambler" telephone system was also set up to ensure that our calls could not be overheard or monitored by anyone.

When we were set up with office equipment, David Young moved into the principal sub-office behind Kathy Chenow's desk with windows facing Seventeenth Street and East Executive Drive. A large conference table was set up in the center sub-office, and it was here that we held our first meeting as a team on July 23. It had taken less than a week to assemble the team and the facilities that would become known as "the Plumbers." Staffing of the group was now complete: we were Bud Krogh, Gordon Liddy, Howard Hunt, David Young, and Kathy Chenow.

At the beginning of our first meeting we discussed how Ehrlichman had described the assignment. I emphasized that the president viewed our work as critical to America's national security and that we would be operating with full support from senior staff and from the president. We were to leave no stone unturned in our investigation of the leak of the top-secret Pentagon Papers to the *New York Times*. Specifically, we needed to determine Ellsberg's reason for releasing the papers and the identity of his collaborators. Had he leaked these documents alone or with the help of a small group? Was he part of a larger conspiracy? We needed to assess the likelihood that he had access to other top-secret information related to President Nixon's secret plans for ending the Vietnam War and if so, determine whether he would be likely to leak this information as well.

One of the unit's first acts was to request "damage assessments" from the CIA and the FBI that they might have prepared about the disclosure of the Pentagon Papers. These assessments would give the unit some understanding of the impacts of the leak on U.S. intelligence systems, methods, and operations. In response to this request, the CIA provided a damage assessment it had prepared before the SIU was set up.

The CIA's assessment reported grounds to believe that a full set of the Pentagon Papers had reached the Soviet embassy in Washington, D.C., before the *New York Times* started publishing its versions on June 13, 1971. Right after the SIU was set up, the FBI provided corroborating intelligence that a full set of the Pentagon Papers had indeed reached the Soviet embassy ahead of publication in the *Times*. We knew, however, that the *Times* had received only a partial set of the Pentagon Papers. This intelligence, raw and unconfirmed though it was, heightened our suspicion that Ellsberg or one of his collaborators, if he had any, may have had some sort of foreign involvement.

Hunt told us that from this damage assessment and other information he had seen to date, it was not unlikely that Ellsberg had some type of Soviet involvement. The Soviet Union was a major supplier of war matériel to the North Vietnamese. Soviet-built radar systems tracked American planes, Soviet surface-to-air missiles shot them down, and the AK–47 was the rifle used by the Vietcong and the North Vietnamese Army to kill American soldiers. It was not a stretch of logic to assume that the Soviet Union would support public release of the Pentagon Papers to rally more public opinion in opposition to the Vietnam War. Moreover, Hunt suggested that any information linking Ellsberg with the Soviets, either directly or indirectly, could be used to discredit Ellsberg and thus undermine any credibility he might have in the public arena.

After our first meeting, a mood of manic resolve to carry out our duties drove us forward. The unit had been given a critical responsibility by the president, and we were embarking on a quest that held great import for the security of the nation. I was confident that we all agreed that Ellsberg was very likely at the center of a Soviet-sponsored conspiracy to diminish U.S. influence in the critical theater of Vietnam. It was an easy conclusion to reach, somehow made all the easier by the complete lack of corroborating evidence. Any doubts we might have nurtured were quickly dispelled; indeed, the unit's high level of resolve and spirit of urgency were vastly increased by the next leak of top-secret information, the subject of my meeting with the president and John Ehrlichman in the Oval Office on July 24, 1971.

CHAPTER 3

A New Leak
for the Plumbers

On Saturday, July 24, 1971, around 10:00 A.M., Ehrlichman called me and said that the president wanted to see us immediately. He told me to drop whatever I was doing and come over and meet him outside the Oval Office. The president had been informed about a story by William Beecher that had just run the day before in the *New York Times* in which he revealed the fallback position of the United States in the first Strategic Arms Limitation Talks (SALT 1) in Helsinki. Ehrlichman said that the president was very, very angry.

Since publication of the story the day before, I had been in regular contact with Al Haig, the deputy national security adviser, regarding who might have leaked the top-secret information to Beecher. Haig told me that he had received some initial information from his contacts at the Department of Defense (DOD) on possible suspects who had access to the top-secret information and who might have had contacts with Beecher. He said that officials in the DOD general counsel's office were investigating and following up on every lead. I learned later that Haig had shared this same information with Ehrlichman.

The headline of the Beecher story was "U.S. Urges Soviet to Join in a Missiles Moratorium," and the sub-headline was, "Would Halt Construction of Land and Sea Arms and Allow Each Nation Up to 300 Antimissile Weapons." The story detailed the elements of proposals that were being considered by the U.S. side for presentation at the SALT 1 talks between the Soviet Union and the United States. The story set out some "ambitious proposals" that the U.S. negotiators were considering privately but that had not yet been developed into specific draft language to present to the Soviets. It also contained specific information from the still-secret American proposals regarding the choice each nation could make "between defending its capital with 100 antiballistic missiles or employing up to 300 defensive missiles, at three sites, to defend offensive missiles."

I had read the Beecher article carefully, but I wasn't familiar with the components of the American proposal and I was not at all informed about the complex and murky arcana of the technical aspects of the SALT 1 talks. Leadership for determining the U.S. positions in the SALT 1 talks was assigned to Kissinger and the National Security Council, with technical support from the DOD and the Arms Control and Disarmament Agency (ACDA). Specifically, Kissinger provided policy guidance to Dr. Gerard Smith, the director of ACDA and the principal negotiator for the United States in Helsinki. I was well aware—as I believe were most White House staff members—that success in the SALT 1 negotiations with the Soviets was considered by the president and Kissinger one of the most critical foreign policy objectives and national security programs that the Nixon administration had launched. On the same day President Nixon was inaugurated, January 20, 1969, the Soviet Foreign Ministry had indicated its interest in pursuing strategic arms limitation discussions with the United States. The president indicated his support for the talks immediately thereafter.

The survival of the planet was potentially at stake in the effort to control the increase of nuclear weapons on the part of both the United States and the Soviet Union. A deal with the Soviets in which both sides would implicitly reject the idea of using nuclear weapons and reduce their nuclear arsenals was to me the ultimate national security imperative.

In 1971 the Soviet Union was still a formidable power, and the cold war was still cold. Even though the SALT 1 talks reflected a gradual thawing, the United States was still engaged in high-stakes military competition with the Soviet Union. Each country possessed sufficient nuclear weapons to annihilate the other. Mutual assured destruction (MAD) was the Armageddon prospect that kept each country from risking its own self-destruction. The purpose of SALT 1 was to reduce the number of nuclear weapons each side could have so that the risk of nuclear war could be correspondingly reduced. I realized on first reading the Beecher article that a leak of this kind was obviously going to be of great concern to the president, and I was right.

After Ehrlichman rang off, I grabbed my yellow pad, rushed out of my office, and speed-walked across West Executive Drive to the West Wing. When I arrived at the secretary's desk outside the Oval Office, Ehrlichman was already there. We waited for only a few seconds, and then the secretary told us to go in.

I followed Ehrlichman into the Oval Office. As we approached the president's desk, I felt the chill and tightening in my gut that I always felt when going into a meeting with him. Each president redecorates the Oval Office according to his taste, and I always found Richard Nixon's Oval Office stark, cold, and austere. To the right of his massive desk, five service flags stood sentinel, each flag topped by a golden eagle. A black phone sat on the left side of the president's desk. Two chairs upholstered in gold abutted the desk on the right and left sides. A collection of ceramic birds were perched on wall shelves on either side of the door to the president's private office. Apart from the presidential seal that hung on the wall just to the left of the door to the Secret Service agent's station—it had been embroidered by Julie Nixon Eisenhower during the campaign and given to her father when he had "gone over the top" to win the 1968 election—there wasn't a square centimeter of space in the Oval Office that was warm, intimate, or inviting. A large oval blue rug ringed with gold stars covered the floor. A large eagle was woven into the center of the blue rug, and another was emblazoned in the plaster of the ceiling. Two couches faced each other antagonistically in front of an empty fireplace.

I realized later that Nixon's choice of trappings was intended in part to intimidate visitors, particularly those from other countries, with the power and majesty of his presidency. It was no wonder that the president had set up a much warmer and more comfortable private office in the Old Executive Office Building where he could relax, think, and write.

The president was pacing behind his desk, and his mood was obvious: he was extremely upset and very angry. His face was darkly flushed, and he didn't smile at either of us when we got close to his desk. According to the transcript of this meeting, there was an "inaudible section" when it started. This was when the president was still pacing and Ehrlichman and I had not yet sat down in our chairs by his desk. The president said that he was not going to stand for Beecher-type leaks anymore. He slammed his right fist into his open left hand to emphasize his point. I told him that we had some information about the potential leaker in the Department of Defense and that we were considering administering a polygraph test to this suspect. The president then waved us to the chairs next to his desk (and thus within the reach of the bugs embedded in that desk), and our meeting continued.

After I told him about a suspect for the leak, the president said, "I think that's a place to start. Hook this guy. Hit it very hard, consider it [a] true fight." I mentioned the possibility of polygraphing this suspect, and the president said, "Take it over. And then immediately get a confession from him. Start with him."

Ehrlichman then cautioned the president that, in Al Haig's opinion, if we proceeded with the polygraphs and the pressure we were sure to get resignations and legal action. We discussed polygraphing twenty or thirty people. While the transcript indicates that either Ehrlichman or I said, "Fine. Start there and let's screw the hell out of that guy and the people around him in that unit," in fact this was the president's comment. Ehrlichman then summarized the status of our investigation thus far:

> Well, we've got one person, that comes out of DOD according to Al Haig, who is the prime suspect right now, a man by the name of Van Cleeve who they feel is very much the guy that did it. Spent two hours with Beecher apparently this week, he had access to the documents. Uh, he apparently had views very similar to those which were reflected in the Beecher article, and it would be my feeling that we should begin with him, and go immediately around him before going to a dragnet polygraph of any other people.

After the president agreed that we should start with Van Cleeve, Ehrlichman suggested that polygraphs should follow if Van Cleeve turned out not to be the one. The president asked whether any of these potential leakers were more hawkish or dovish, to which Ehrlichman responded that Haig couldn't tell us anything about that at this point. The president responded, "I don't care whether he's a hawk or a dove or anything. Now that the thing's leaked, he's up with the government."

The president then said, after discussing whether a million people had top-secret clearances, "Here's what I want. . . . Little people do not leak. This crap . . . this crap is never-ending. I studied these cases long enough, and it's always the son of a bitch that leaks. . . ."

"Ellsberg," I put in, nodding, and repeated, "Ellsberg!"

"Sure," the president responded. "So, what I would like to do is have everybody down through GS-something-or-other, you know, the Foreign Service . . . you know what I mean . . . ? Here in Washington I want all of them who have top-secret clearances . . . to take part. And then I think maybe another approach would be to set up a . . . classification, all right, which we would call what?"

We brainstormed possible classifications that could protect the most sensitive information that the president deemed important. The president ruled out using the word *presidential* in any classification scheme, saying, "Don't use my . . . goddamn office." He then suggested a number of possibilities for the new classification scheme. He continued: "So we'll know what people had it. Now, the fact that a hundred had it . . . I want to find out why a hundred had it."

Before I had been assigned to codirect the SIU with David Young on July 16, a program had been launched within the national security apparatus of the government to declassify information that had no real justification for being classified. I learned that one of the principal reasons classified information was leaked was the antiquated and unworkable classification system. So much information was classified that it was almost impossible to maintain the secrecy of the information that was truly sensitive and dangerous if disclosed. The president then told Ehrlichman and me that the declassification group should have been done with its work already. "Well, goddamn it, I told them two weeks ago . . . they should follow up on it. Nobody at all is up on a goddamned thing. We've got to follow up on this thing, however."

Ehrlichman answered, "They're going to come back at you with a whole new classification scheme."

The president shot back angrily, "But they didn't. But they didn't." Trying to respond to the president's dissatisfaction with the pace of the declassification work and to inject some realism into our discussion, I said quietly that it would take a while longer to develop a new classification scheme.

The president then circled back to polygraphing. He said that we had to limit the number of people who had access to the most sensitive national security information. After searching again for a useful descriptor—"national security . . . with three letters like FM or SMS"—the president said that everyone who received this information "must sign an agreement to take a polygraph. . . . [W]ith regard to the agreement to take a polygraph pledge: I want that to be done now, with about four or five hundred people in State, Defense . . . so that we can immediately enter that. Don't you figure that?"

"Yes, I do," answered Ehrlichman.

I then added, "Yes, sir, we're going to have drafts of that waiver prepared and stamps, we're going to have to look at what the stamps [of the new classification will state]."

The president then targeted the people and agencies to be covered by the new system: "the top executives of the government . . . that should include everybody on the NSC staff, for example. You start with them. You should include about a hundred people. . . . Probably four or five hundred at State, four or five hundred at Defense, and . . . two or three hundred over at . . . CIA . . . that's it. I don't care about these other agencies. All CIA people have gone through a polygraph."

After laying out his target groups, the president said, "I don't know anything about polygraphs, and I don't know how accurate they are, but I know they'll scare the hell out of people."

I agreed with the president that polygraphs usually scared people because they asked a lot of personal questions. But I said that the upcoming polygraphs would focus much more specifically on a few questions about the Beecher story and contacts with him. Ehrlichman added that we would follow up on Haig's advice to focus on Van Cleeve.

Ehrlichman then promised that we would work on it through the weekend and send anything we found to the president. Nixon made it clear that he would be available, day or night.

Ehrlichman added, "All right, I just wanted to know. And if we catch the guy, and his resignation is to be demanded . . . "

The president then hunched forward, sliced the air with his hand, and said angrily, "Not quiet. All right, understand. . . . You catch anybody, it's not going to be quiet. I'm gonna, we're gonna put the goddamn story out. He's going to be dismissed, prosecuted. . . ."

Ehrlichman cautioned again, "Uh, the polygraph is not useful for prosecution."

The president retorted, "All right, but the point is that if a charge is made against him, that we're going to have to see that he's to be prosecuted. . . . I'll let you work the guy out."

The president then looked directly at me and said, "All right?" I nodded. He then said, with his voice rising, "This does affect the national security, this is a case for measures . . . like the Pentagon Papers. This would involve the current negotiation, and it should not [be] getting out, jeopardiz[ing] . . . the negotiation position." He then pointed at me and almost shouted, "Now, goddamn it, we're not going to allow that. We're just not going to allow it." He then dismissed me with a wave and a cursory "Good luck."

Once the president rose from his chair and it was clear that he had concluded the meeting, Ehrlichman and I got up to leave. The president indicated that he wanted to talk with Ehrlichman alone as he headed toward the door leading out to the Rose Garden and to Marine One, the president's helicopter. It had been idling on the south lawn for most of our meeting, ready to take the president to Camp David.

As I walked out of the Oval Office, I felt an overwhelming sense of personal responsibility to take whatever action might be necessary to stop the kinds of leaks that were imperiling the president's negotiations. By directly connecting the Pentagon Papers and SALT 1 leaks to their effect on national security, Nixon made me feel even more that my assignment was of utmost importance. As I understood it, I was engaged in protecting two of the paramount national security objectives of the times: reducing the threat of nuclear war by a successful negotiation with the Soviet Union in the SALT 1 talks, and minimizing the negative effect of the release of the Pentagon Papers on the president's policy for ending the Vietnam War.

At that time I did not scrutinize the level of threat these two leaks posed to national security. The very words "national security" served to block critical analysis. The most basic definition of the term "national security" is the broad set of policies, programs, and activities that protect the survival of the nation. It seemed at the very least presumptuous, if not unpatriotic, for me to inquire into just what the significance of national security was in those two leaks. For me to suggest that national security was being improperly invoked would have been to invite a confrontation with both patriotism and loyalty. That kind of confrontation was well beyond what I was capable of at the time.

CHAPTER 4

Sparring with the CIA, the FBI, and "Deep Throat"

O nce out of the Oval Office, I rushed back to my office in the EOB, sat down, and called Liddy and Young. Liddy was in room 16 that Saturday morning, but Young was not. I took a circuitous route down two halls of the EOB and down one flight of stairs to room 16. Like other members of the unit, I tried to keep both the existence of room 16 and the fact that I worked there on occasion as confidential as I could. When I knocked on the door, Liddy opened it quickly. I walked in, asked him to join me in the conference room, and explained what had just happened.

I gave him a detailed account of my meeting with the president and Ehrlichman and explained that the work of the unit had been officially expanded by the commander in chief to cover the SALT 1 leak of the day before. I stressed that I had never been in a meeting with the president where he was so incredibly angry.

When Liddy asked specifically how the president felt and what he had said, I answered that he looked flushed and very disturbed.

The president had punched and sliced the air with his hands and fists, using several "goddamns" to emphasize his points. I told Liddy that the president had placed the responsibility for not allowing any more of these leaks squarely on me and our team. His final order was that we were to go after the SALT 1 leak with the same no-holds-barred measures we were using in investigating Ellsberg and the leak of the Pentagon Papers. The SIU was now operating with a whole new sense of mission.

I needed to arrange immediately for the polygraphs that the president wanted, starting that day and continuing through the weekend. My first call was to the director of central intelligence (DCI), Richard Helms. In about five minutes, the White House operator located him on a tennis court. Like all DCIs, Helms was never more than a few minutes away from phone contact with his agency and the White House.

When he came on the line a little breathless, I explained to him that I had just come from a meeting with the president, who was furious about the leak of the SALT 1 fallback negotiating position in William Beecher's *New York Times* article the day before. I told him that the president wasn't going to "allow" this to continue and that he had ordered us to conduct polygraph tests right away on officials who might have had access to our negotiating positions. I asked him if he could provide machines and operators to get started on these polygraph tests.

Helms quietly heard me out. He then told me in clear, unequivocal language that he had neither the polygraph machines nor the trained operators who could be pulled into service on such short notice. He explained that while the CIA regularly conducted polygraphs of its employees, these tests weren't something that could be pulled together quickly. While he was affable and sounded like he would have liked to help, Helms nevertheless was giving me a firm brush-off.

Although I was disappointed in Helms's response, I wasn't surprised. As we had just advised the president, the information we had received to that point indicated that the likely source of the leak was a Department of Defense official. Through his own intelligence, Helms may have already been aware of the same likelihood.

The relationship between DOD and the CIA, then as now, was often acrimonious and bitter. Helms may have been unwilling to exacerbate the interagency rivalry by lending CIA assets to a hunt for a DOD leaker, which DOD could have construed as an attack. I had been in meetings where representatives of DOD and the CIA disagreed with each other and where, like poised scorpions, they would circle each other waiting for an opportunity to strike. The relationship between the FBI and the CIA was even worse. They often wouldn't even talk to each other, let alone share intelligence. Or Helms may have just realized that a high-pressure request from an intense young White House aide on a Saturday morning wasn't the kind of careful, well-thought-through request that should be honored.

As part of my international narcotics control work, I had developed good working relationships with a few CIA officials and station chiefs in Burma and Laos, but I had not had regular dealings with Helms. My memory of Dick Helms is of a man of razor-sharp intelligence, patrician bearing, and a steely resolve to keep the Agency out of trouble in the internecine agency wars that were waged in the Nixon administration. He also would go to great lengths, including false declarations before Congress, to keep the secrets of the CIA. He was the consummate gentleman spy. So in spite of being disappointed to some degree in Helms's response, I didn't belabor it or indicate any dissatisfaction to him.

My next call was to the director of the Federal Bureau of Investigation, J. Edgar Hoover. It wasn't always easy to make contact with the director, even with a call from the White House on behalf of the president. One of my responsibilities on the White House staff was to act as liaison between the Bureau and the White House on law enforcement issues designated by Ehrlichman. I also dealt with policy issues such as Bureau staffing at home and in U.S. embassies abroad, and specifically how the federal government should respond to antiwar protests and civil disorders.

For the first few months of the Nixon administration, as staff assistant to the counsel to the president, I had also been entrusted with reading and evaluating all of the FBI full field investigation reports on nominees to key federal positions in the departments and agencies. Even though I was assigned to read these personal, sensitive documents, I was not in the loop on the more secret national security wiretaps that were requested from the FBI by Bob Haldeman and John Ehrlichman. Targets included the media and national security staff. These wiretap requests were usually made with the knowledge and endorsement of Dr. Kissinger and the president. I did know that Hoover had a direct communication link with the president, but I was not privy to either the substance or the frequency of those contacts. As a result of this compartmentalization of White House staff responsibilities, no one had a complete, overall picture of the critical relationship between the Bureau and the White House. When I was asked to arrange a meeting for the president and Hoover, it was always necessary for me to get several open times on the president's schedule and offer them to the director so that he could determine when it was convenient for him to come to the White House. In those days in the twilight of Hoover's career, it was commonly assumed that he had amassed a tremendous amount of confidential and potentially damaging information on practically everyone of consequence in the government. This knowledge instilled fear in many people. No one wanted to risk offending Hoover.

On that Saturday morning, July 24, I was successful in getting through to Hoover very quickly. As I had done with Helms, I explained what had just happened in my meeting with the president. Hoover listened carefully. He said that he thought the Bureau might have a polygraph machine and an operator available. But under no circumstances could a test be done over the weekend. And he was talking about one test, not several, as the president had preferred.

I knew that it took time, sometimes days, to set up a polygraph test, to formulate the questions, and to prepare both the administrator and the test-taker. I had just told the president that in any polygraph tests we initiated we would limit the questions to the circumstances surrounding the SALT 1 leak, particularly the question of who had access to William Beecher and what was said between them. I repeated this to Hoover. He said that he would work with us, and when I told him that I was going to set up a meeting that afternoon to discuss how to proceed, he said that he would send Mark Felt, the number-three man in the Bureau, to attend the meeting. I thanked him and rang off.

Liddy had called Hunt and asked him to join us in room 16. I briefed Hunt on the events and calls of that morning and requested that he and Liddy join me in the meeting that afternoon to pursue the SALT investigation further. I then called Bob Mardian, the assistant attorney general for internal security, and invited him to the meeting along with Mark Felt. I also invited J. Fred Buzhardt, the general counsel of the DOD, who had been assigned to investigate the DOD leak.

The meeting started early Saturday afternoon in the Roosevelt Room. This room is a large, elegant meeting place directly across from the Oval Office in the West Wing. As associate director of the Domestic Council and deputy assistant to the president, I met in the Roosevelt Room weekdays at 7:30 A.M. when Congress was in session. These meetings were attended by my colleagues on the Domestic Council, senior staff from the Office of Management and Budget (OMB), and the White House congressional relations staff. Serious discussions on current policy issues occurred daily, and major decisions were made in the Roosevelt Room. The famous painting of Theodore Roosevelt leading the charge up San Juan Hill in the Spanish-American War hung on the north wall, enhancing the room's sense of history. I wanted to impress upon Mardian, Felt, and Buzhardt that the SALT leak was a matter of grave importance to the president. Meeting in the Roosevelt Room would underscore the gravity of the situation.

A description of this meeting in the Roosevelt Room was included in an article by John O'Conner in the July 2005 issue of *Vanity Fair* entitled "I'm the Guy They Called Deep Throat." O'Conner, the author of the article and a sometime lawyer for Mark Felt's family, includes Felt's account of this meeting:

> Well before Hoover's death, relations between the Nixon camp and the FBI deteriorated. In 1971, Felt was called to 1600 Pennsylvania Avenue. The President, Felt was told, had begun "climbing the walls" because someone (a government insider, Nixon believed) was leaking details to *The New York Times* about the administration's strategy for upcoming arms talks with the Soviets. Nixon's aides wanted the Bureau to find the culprit, either through wiretaps or by insisting that suspects submit to lie-detector tests. Such leaks led the White House to begin employing ex-CIA types to do their own, homespun spying, creating its nefarious "Plumbers" unit, to which the Watergate cadre belonged.
>
> Felt arrived at the White House to confront an odd gathering. Egil "Bud" Krogh, Jr., deputy assistant to the President for domestic affairs, presided, and attendees included ex-spy E.

Howard Hunt and Robert Mardian, an assistant Attorney General—"a balding little man," Felt recalled, "dressed in what looked like work clothes and dirty tennis shoes . . . shuffling about the room, arranging the chairs and I [first] took him to be a member of the cleaning staff." (Mardian had been summoned to the West Wing from a weekend tennis game.) According to Felt, once the meeting began, Felt expressed resistance to the idea of wiretapping suspected leakers without a court order.

After the session, which ended with no clear resolution, Krogh's group began to have reason to suspect a single Pentagon employee. Nixon, nonetheless, demanded that "four or five hundred people in State, Defense, and so forth [also be polygraphed] so that we can immediately scare the bastards." Two days later, as Felt wrote in his book, he was relieved when Krogh told him that the Administration had decided to let "the Agency," not the FBI, "handle the polygraph interviews. . . . Obviously, John Ehrlichman [Krogh's boss, Nixon's top domestic-policy adviser, and the head of the Plumbers unit] had decided to 'punish' the Bureau for what he saw as its lack of cooperation and its refusal to get involved in the work which the 'Plumbers' later undertook."

The real story was somewhat different. First, I thanked the men for coming to the White House on such short notice. All of them, unlike Liddy and me, were in their weekend clothes. I emphasized that the president wanted us to pursue an individual in the Department of Defense as aggressively as we could over the weekend and that this might require one or several lie detector tests. I did not mention placing a wiretap without a warrant as part of the investigation. So there was no need for Mark Felt to express "resistance to the idea of wiretapping suspected leakers without a court order." I stayed within the framework of pushing for fairly widespread polygraphs of leak suspects that I had just discussed two hours earlier with the president and Ehrlichman.

On July 24, I had not yet determined that the FBI was not committed to helping the SIU aggressively pursue leak investigations. That came later. So I had no predisposition that day to be critical of the Bureau or to want to "punish" them two days later. It may well be that Mark Felt lumped together some of his meetings later with junior White House staff members with this meeting on the SALT 1 leak on July 24. I had met with Felt on several occasions and always found him to be a very classy man, smart, competent, and ready to help. It seems odd that Felt would include this meeting as one in a series of meetings in which young White House staff members abused their authority or were trying to damage the Bureau, thus justifying his later decision to provide Watergate investigative material to Bob Woodward, who originated Felt's nickname "Deep Throat" for his colleagues on the *Washington Post* staff.

I did, however, repeat some of the president's strong language about what we were to do so that the FBI would share the sense of urgency that had been impressed on me. We left the meeting with the understanding that the FBI would take steps to make a polygraph machine and operator available early the following week if we needed it. Fred Buzhardt was to continue leading the investigation at the Department of Defense, which had already shown some promise. At the end of the meeting I reiterated the president's parting language to me about our responsibility to ferret out the leaker and to stop further leaks: "Goddamn it, we're not going to allow that. We're just not going to allow it."

CHAPTER 5

A Proposal
Gone Awry

After the meeting in the Roosevelt Room, I confirmed with Al Haig that he would monitor Buzhardt's investigation at the DOD. David Young agreed to track the follow-up work with Haig. If the DOD investigation was successful in identifying the individual who leaked the SALT I fallback position, the dragnet type of polygraphing that the president was so adamant in pushing could be avoided. With that investigative course under way, I set about with Young to prepare the SIU team for further work.

We had been given direct orders from the president to get to the bottom of both the Ellsberg case and the SALT 1 leak, and this work would require us to be able to read highly classified and sensitive information. Our unit was also tasked with finding out whether the Kennedy administration had been somehow involved in the assassination of President Diem in South Vietnam in 1963, part of the president's ongoing preoccupation with uncovering wrongdoing and incompetence in earlier administrations. Another area of interest for the president was the Kennedy administration's disastrous handling of the Bay of Pigs invasion in

Cuba. To carry out all of these highly sensitive investigations, we concluded that we would need clearances from the initiating agencies to read some of the most sensitive, highly classified memoranda and back-channel cable traffic.

At this time in the Plumbers' operation, I wasn't able to differentiate between matters of national security and matters that were primarily political. My inability to clearly delineate these considerations may have been influenced by the president, who had conflated his views on his own political survival and well-being with his idea of a national security imperative. We certainly didn't take the time to analyze what could appropriately be done by the president as commander in chief under the Constitution, what he could do as head of the executive branch, and what he could do as the political leader of his party and future candidate for a second term of office. We simply charged forward without thinking about these critical distinctions. To do our work we needed higher security clearances.

As a requirement for our respective jobs in Treasury (Liddy), the CIA (Hunt), and the White House (Young and myself), we had already received clearances to read classified information up to and including top-secret information. As Kissinger's personal aide, Young had already received clearances higher than top-secret, including some of the most sensitive classified clearances in the U.S. government. Liddy and I needed these additional clearances to handle the material for our work. Before we could get them, the CIA sent a man to brief us on these higher levels of security information. After showing us his identification, he explained the highly sensitive nature of this classified information, which could be accessed only with appropriate code words. After showing us some of the highly sensitive information we then had access to, including incredibly clear satellite-acquired photographs of people and vehicles, the CIA briefer solemnly administered confidentiality oaths to us. We signed papers promising never to disclose this type of information in the future.

With the CIA security briefing behind us, we were now cleared to handle the classified information of most concern to the unit. First, however, we needed to "harden" the security of room 16 to ensure that other White House staff members, wandering visitors, or occasional media representatives did not gain access to it. We needed a safe place to meet and maintain our files. To this end, we sent a request through Bob Haldeman's office, and through that office to the technical services division of the Secret Service, to install a motion-detector system in room 16 that would detect any unauthorized intruder. The system was up and running within two days of our request. Unfortunately, the system was so sensitive that if a paper floated off the top of a file because of a change in pressure in the ventilation system, an alarm would ring in the Secret Service command post in the EOB and an armed agent would run down to check on the office. Several false alarms brought agents to check up on errant flying documents. We were encouraged to make sure everything in room 16 was stowed safely away at the end of each day before we armed the system for its night's work.

On July 29, 1971, the president sent a letter to FBI director Hoover, at the request of Young and me, advising him that I had been directed to examine in depth the circumstances of the many disclosures of top-secret and other sensitive information to the public. Young, Liddy, and I felt that unless the president weighed in with Hoover, we were unlikely to get the kind of aggressive investigation the president wanted. In a letter to me dated August 3, 1971, Hoover acknowledged the president's letter. He attached the results of five completed interviews with individuals named in a list of seventeen persons identified in an attachment to the president's letter. He also included a background paper on Daniel

Ellsberg that we had requested. Hoover asked for my concurrence to conduct the remaining interviews, except for Ellsberg, which I granted. All of the enclosures were classified. This August 3 letter from Hoover didn't exhibit the urgency we felt was necessary.

In a meeting of the SIU during the week of July 26, Liddy, Young, and I had asked ourselves whether the Bureau was proceeding on a "Bureau special" basis, as they were supposed to be doing. A Bureau special involved a major commitment of resources in the FBI, and we weren't sure the Ellsberg/Pentagon Papers investigation was receiving that commitment. Lots of paper flowed to us from the Bureau, but that didn't mean an aggressive investigation was really under way. Liddy took on the task of finding out. In his career with the FBI, Liddy knew the difference between a normal FBI investigation and one that had the full support of Hoover and his principal deputies. He told us what it was like to be on a Bureau special investigation, and what we were seeing from the Bureau didn't seem to be one.

In meetings Liddy set up with his Bureau contacts during the weeks of July 26 and August 2, he learned that the Bureau was definitely not proceeding on any kind of special basis. Liddy's report to us about this deficiency was an important factor in the self-help mentality that then began to emerge in the unit. Rather than questioning the Bureau's lack of support, we resolved to go forward on our own with the investigation.

Liddy's memorandum of August 2, 1971, detailed his conversation with William Sullivan, the assistant director of the FBI, who led Liddy to believe that there was a general breakdown of capacity within the Bureau. Although I wondered whether Sullivan might have been trying to curry favor with the White House, hoping to succeed Hoover, I considered him to be a credible and reliable person. This memo was forwarded to Ehrlichman and then to the president. A copy found its way to the attorney general and then to Robert Mardian. Overall, the memorandum was a scathing indictment of Bureau practices and the failure of leadership under Hoover.

Liddy's memo was prepared right at the time when Congressman Hale Boggs (D-La.) leveled an attack against Hoover and the Bureau and called for a congressional investigation. According to another report from Liddy, Deputy Attorney General Richard Kleindienst's initial support for a congressional investigation of the FBI was shut down when Hoover called the president to let him know that, if called to testify, he would be forced to testify about "all" he knew about the Bureau's national security investigations. I understood this to mean that Hoover would disclose the warrantless wiretaps that the Bureau had implemented at White House insistence before the SIU was created. The congressional investigation did not go forward. Liddy's report further undermined my confidence that the Bureau could be trusted to carry forward the Pentagon Papers investigation effectively. If Hoover was willing to blackmail the president to avoid embarrassment, we asked ourselves, what else might he be prepared to do if he got crosswise with the White House?

The SIU members felt that we needed an assessment of Ellsberg's mental state to help us determine the likelihood that he would release other classified information. We had determined that as an employee at the Rand Corporation, a major defense contractor, Ellsberg probably had access to a wide assortment of classified documents. We were concerned that he might have had access to Nixon's current Vietnam War plans (from 1969 to 1971), which contained some of the most sensitive information in the government. We also felt that a psychological profile would provide fuel to discredit Ellsberg.

Obtaining information that could be used to discredit Ellsberg was the specific assignment of Hunt, who was reporting directly to Colson. Colson was the White House staff lead on getting derogatory information on any topic into the public arena, either through congressional hearings or through friendly reporters. The grist of the information that the unit felt could discredit Ellsberg was any connection with the Soviet Union.

Ellsberg had been seeing a psychiatrist by the name of Dr. Lewis Fielding for a number of years. Without knowing that psychiatrists rarely keep written notes about their patients (an "oh no, you're kidding me" type of fact that I learned from Jerry Jaffe, my White House colleague and best psychiatrist friend, long after the Pentagon Papers case was resolved), the unit assumed that the files maintained by Fielding would yield a treasure trove of information about Ellsberg. These might even include indications from Ellsberg that he was allied in some way with individuals who were giving information to the KGB and working on behalf of the Soviet Union. When we asked the FBI for the results of its interview with Fielding in early August, we were told that no information was available. Fielding had quite properly refused on the grounds of doctor-patient privilege to reveal any information about Ellsberg to the Bureau.

The CIA psychological profile of Ellsberg that we had requested from the Agency turned out to be shallow and unsatisfactory. Even though Young had explained to the Agency the importance we placed on getting in-depth information, nothing came back that was of any use. We had struck out working through both the FBI and the CIA. The self-help attitude that we were all feeling now ripened into a serious proposal.

In a meeting of all members of the unit, we discussed the steps we felt we could take to get the background we needed on Ellsberg. It was then, during the first week of August, that the idea of a covert operation first surfaced. The idea originated with either Liddy or Hunt.

In one of our planning sessions in room 16, Liddy explained to Young and me that he had been directly involved in several so-called black bag jobs as an FBI agent. He knew firsthand about several covert operations that had involved entering foreign embassies and consulates for the purpose of acquiring national security information. In these covert national security operations, the FBI would quietly inform the local police about an area surrounding the target embassy or consulate so that they would stay away while the FBI black bag job was being conducted. He told us that these operations were carried out when the national security interests were very strong. Given the president's clear directive that we were working on a matter of the highest national security importance, and with his charge to us to move forward with all resources available, we felt that a covert operation would be necessary and defensible. During deliberations, no one in the SIU questioned the necessity, legitimacy, legality, or morality of our proposed covert operation.

It was in this context that on August 11 Young drafted and I cosigned a memorandum to Ehrlichman. We recommended in paragraph two of our memo that "a covert operation be undertaken to examine all the medical files still held by Ellsberg's psychoanalyst covering the two-year period in which he was undergoing analysis." In the line below the recommendation, we set out two potential responses: "Approve_____ Disapprove_____." Ehrlichman wrote his initial "E" after "Approve" and then wrote in longhand beneath his approval: "if done under your assurance that it is not traceable."

The fifth paragraph, a section that was redacted in most copies of this memorandum because of national security concerns, recommended that contacts be made with MI–5, the British government's counter-espionage agency, to determine whether that agency had "overheard" (wiretapped) Ellsberg at any time during his student days at Cambridge. Hunt felt that it was plausible that Ellsberg might have been "turned" by Soviet intelligence while a Cambridge student. He explained that a few brilliant British students, Kim Philby in particular, had been brought into the Soviet fold while studying at Cambridge. They had risen to high positions in government and British society as they became notorious spies for the Soviet Union. In Hunt's view, it was clearly in the interest of the Soviets to undermine the U.S. war effort in Vietnam.

Ellsberg was obviously a brilliant man and had been a brilliant student at Harvard and Cambridge. If he had been "turned" as a student, it would help explain how he had arranged a transfer of a full set of the Pentagon Papers to the Soviet embassy before they were published by the *New York Times*. (To this day, we don't know for sure if the Soviet embassy received its own copy of the Pentagon Papers before the *New York Times* did, and if so, how.) According to Hunt, proof that he had colluded with the Soviets would have gone far to discredit Ellsberg personally and undermine his standing as a moral antiwar activist. My reading of the Hiss case in *Six Crises*, which recounts Nixon's success in proving Hiss's involvement in a Soviet spy ring, inspired this speculative track of thinking among our unit's members and helps explain why this recommendation was included in the August 11 memorandum.

With Ehrlichman's approval of the covert operation recommended in paragraph two of the August 11 memorandum, the wheels were set in motion to carry it out. We did not analyze any of the potential consequences of this operation, and we did not comprehend that we were sowing poisonous seeds that would eventually deform the Nixon administration, leading to its eventual demise.

As soon as I received Ehrlichman's approval in the memo, I called a meeting with Liddy, Hunt, and Young. We laid out the steps that we needed to take to put together a successful covert operation to examine Fielding's psychiatric files about Ellsberg.

We agreed that it would be necessary to undertake a reconnaissance mission to evaluate the obstacles to getting into Fielding's office in a complex in Beverly Hills. Because Ehrlichman had specifically directed that the operation not be traceable, I felt that it would require operatives who had no direct contact with White House staff.

Hunt informed us that he had worked closely with a team of Cuban Americans in his capacity as an agent with the CIA, starting with the Bay of Pigs disaster in 1961. These Cuban Americans had varying degrees of background and experience in CIA operations and methods. Hunt felt that his former colleagues would be willing to help us carry out this operation. First we needed to scope out the area and understand the requirements.

Hunt recommended that we request support from the CIA in performing the reconnaissance. We asked Ehrlichman to contact General Robert Cushman, the deputy director of the CIA, to obtain CIA technical support for the mission and for any follow-up work that might need to be done. That we were openly requesting assistance from the CIA indicated our belief that we were engaged in a legitimate national security investigation and that we weren't playing outside the rules. Even though we knew the CIA didn't have jurisdiction on U.S. soil, we felt that we could still use its equipment without compromising the Agency. Hunt persuaded us that since he and his team would not be working for the CIA, mere use of CIA equipment would not violate the prohibition on Agency activity within the United States.

When he called Cushman, Ehrlichman told him that Hunt had been hired by the White House staff in a security capacity. Ehrlichman asked for Cushman's support for work that Hunt might do as part of the White House staff. The CIA arranged for one of its technical specialists to meet Hunt and Liddy in a D.C. safe house. Both were given an alias and documentation, and Liddy was given a small camera to use in photographing the office area. Hunt and Liddy were also given disguise materials, including an ill-fitting red wig for Hunt and Coke-bottle-thick glasses for Liddy. Liddy also received a gait-altering device.

On August 25, Liddy and Hunt left for California and checked into the Beverly Hilton Hotel. Hunt told me that he wanted to have an individual in California available to the team in case an emergency arose, so he contacted Morton "Tony" Jackson, a Beverly Hills attorney who had worked with Hunt in the CIA. They explained to Jackson that they were conducting a sensitive drug control operation.

The day after meeting with Jackson, Liddy and Hunt went to Fielding's office and surveyed it from many directions, using what they claimed was "good tradecraft." They took photographs of Fielding's building and posed Liddy in the foreground, like a tourist, with the office in the background.

In an example of somewhat less skilled tradecraft, they left the film of Liddy posing in front of Fielding's office in the camera. The camera was returned to the CIA with the incriminating film still inside. Although this appeared to be a major breach in operational security, we were assuming at the time that the CIA was on the same team as the White House staff and would not be looking for ways to undermine a project that had such strong presidential support.

I learned later that inside the CIA there was some grave concern that supporting the SIU could be seen as a CIA violation of the statutory limitations on domestic activities. There was legitimate fear of vulnerability for the Agency if it was associated in some way with clandestine domestic operations.

That same evening, Hunt and Liddy conducted a more thorough reconnaissance of the building. They wanted to understand the clinic crew and the janitors' schedules. Hunt also talked to a Hispanic cleaning woman in Spanish, who opened Dr. Fielding's door for them so that they could photograph the interior. Apparently she believed their story that they were doctors who needed to leave an urgent message for Fielding. After her help, Hunt tipped her. Soon thereafter they left for the airport and returned to D.C.

The CIA technical support person met them at Dulles to pick up the camera and film, which the CIA subsequently developed. Very few of the pictures turned out because of a camera malfunction and low light conditions. However, the photo of Liddy posing in Fielding's parking space came out bright and clear.

Liddy and Hunt formulated an operational plan and gave it to Young and me the day after their return from the reconnaissance mission. Young and I felt that we needed to communicate with Ehrlichman further before we gave the final green light for the break-in. We told Liddy and Hunt that they were not to go into the Fielding office building themselves. Only the Cuban Americans should be directly involved in carrying out the operation.

Hunt then contacted his team, Bernard Barker, Felipe De Diego, and Eugenio Martinez. When I asked Hunt how much it would cost to hire the team, he told me that they would not take compensation beyond their immediate expenses. He explained to them that this operation served the national security of the country. The three of them felt that it was their patriotic duty to support the mission. Hunt also told me that Martinez was a particularly skilled covert operator who had surreptitiously entered Cuba over thirty-five times during the previous ten years. Hunt was pleased that Martinez was on the team to support Barker and De Diego. All three would be prosecuted for their involvement in the Fielding operation.

I asked Hunt and Liddy for the total cost of the operation—plane fare, hotel, equipment. They thought that $2,000 in cash would cover it. I called Colson and told him that we were ready to go forward with an effort to acquire some information about Ellsberg and that I would need some operational money to carry it out. Colson told me that he would get those funds for me and that the money would be delivered by an intermediary sometime the next day.

Two days before the operation, on Wednesday, September 1, there was a knock on the door of a little-used, poorly marked back entrance to my office. I had told Colson that whoever was to deliver the funds was to use that back entrance and not go through the regular entrance where my secretary worked. I also did not want the funds delivered to room 16, which we had kept as secret as we could from other members of the White House staff and other visitors.

I got up from my desk and opened the door a crack. A man I didn't know quietly handed me an envelope, turned around quickly, and left.

The next day Young came to my office for our final communication with Ehrlichman, who was vacationing on Cape Cod with his wife. We put a call through to him and told him that we were ready to "go forward" in California. I kept the conversation general and avoided saying anything specific, owing to the public nature of the phone call. I also assumed that he was familiar enough with the practices of a covert operation that he would understand what we were asking him to approve. I didn't feel that it was necessary to describe the details of the operation in this final communication, in part because we already had his written approval and active involvement in calling the CIA for logistical support. At David Young's request, Ehrlichman had also asked Colson for an outline of how he intended to use the information obtained from

Hunt and Liddy's operation. During the phone call, Ehrlichman confirmed to Young and me that we should go forward and let him know what information we acquired.

Hunt and Liddy were waiting impatiently in room 16 for the money and approval. They were impatient because it was getting close to time to leave and they needed preparation time to conduct the operation that Labor Day weekend. After getting off the phone with Ehrlichman, I took the money to Liddy and told him to make sure that he exchanged the bills for others to prevent any kind of tracing. My instructions to them were to call me at my home in Crystal City as soon as the operation had been completed. I told Liddy and Hunt, "For God's sake, don't get caught."

Over the next two days Liddy and Hunt flew first to Chicago, where they acquired radio transceiver equipment for the entry operation, and then to Los Angeles, using their aliases provided by the CIA. The operation went forward on the evening of Friday, September 3, right before Labor Day weekend. Following the plan they had presented to us, they went to Fielding's office and discovered that the door to the building was locked, despite preparations to make sure it was unlocked. To gain entry, they broke an external window that was shielded by trees, hoping to make it look as if there had been a burglary to steal drugs from a doctor's office. During the search of Fielding's office, the Cuban-American team spread papers and pills around, doing further damage to the office. They took Polaroid pictures of the damage they inflicted.

Their operation turned up no information or files relevant to Daniel Ellsberg.

During the operation I was in my fiber-backed rocking chair in my apartment in Crystal City, Virginia, rocking back and forth and waiting for the call from Liddy. It was well past 1:00 A.M.

EST when Liddy called to report that they had gotten in and out cleanly, but that no mother lode of information about Ellsberg had been found. He promised a full report on his return.

During the time of the operation, I had imagined getting a chilling call from the Beverly Hills Police Department informing me that they had five men under arrest who had given the police my name and telephone number. So I was as relieved as I had ever been in my life to know that they had made it out of the building without getting caught. However, I sensed then but did not fully comprehend that something irrevocable had occurred.

On Sunday, September 5, Hunt and Liddy returned to D.C., but I didn't see Liddy until Tuesday. I met him in room 16, where he showed me the Polaroid photographs of the damage they had inflicted on the office. I was stunned and appalled by what I saw. I couldn't understand what was unclear about the word "covert" in "covert operation." Liddy said that making the operation look like a drug burglary gone awry would make it less traceable to the White House. Liddy showed me the tools and the lethal-looking combat knife that he had carried during the operation. I asked him if he would have used the knife if he or the team seemed threatened; he assured me that he would have killed if necessary. This admission shocked me because I had simply not envisioned any potential violence, particularly violence that could have led to someone's death.

It is true that I wasn't an expert in covert operations and that seeing the evidence of the damage affected me much more strongly than the theory and planning had. That Liddy would have killed somebody if necessary seemed to be far in excess of what Young or I had contemplated. The recognition that the operation could have resulted in such a dire outcome made me deeply question whether we were on the right course. As Liddy pointed out to me later, I was not prepared for the real possibility that a covert operation could result in fatalities. Feeling disappointed by the failure of their mission, Liddy suggested that he and Hunt go back to California to look for Ellsberg's files in Dr. Fielding's home. I was noncommittal and said that I needed to talk to Ehrlichman before giving an answer.

On September 8, I took the photographs to Ehrlichman to report on what had happened. He too seemed shocked and surprised by the extent of the damage in the operation and told me to shut down any further investigation of Ellsberg through covert operations. He added that what he was seeing was beyond the scope of what he had approved. I told him that it was beyond the scope of what I had envisioned too, and I agreed that we ought not to authorize any further covert activity. I returned to room 16 later that day and informed Liddy and Hunt that Ehrlichman had rejected their suggestion about conducting a break-in of Dr. Fielding's apartment. With this decision, my involvement with the covert activities of the Plumbers came to an end.

On September 9, Ehrlichman met with the president and reported to him that we had a "little operation in California" that had netted nothing and that it was better that he not know about it. Then, on September 10, Ehrlichman met with the president and recommended a covert operation into the National Archives. As recounted in *The New Nixon Tapes: Abuse of Power*, Ehrlichman said to the president, "There's a lot of hanky-panky with secret documents, and on the eve of the publication of the Pentagon Papers those three guys [Nitze, Morton Halperin, and Leslie Gelb] made a deposit into the National Archives, under an agreement, of a whole lot of papers. Now I'm going to steal those documents out of the National Archives." After an exchange of ideas about how to do it, Ehrlichman continued, "Yeah. And nobody can tell we've been in there."

In 2007 I learned from John Powers, the director of the Nixon papers at the National Archives, that an operation at the National Archives was in fact carried out. Whoever was responsible for this operation did not work with me in the Plumbers group.

Over the next two months the work of the SIU focused on other leaks besides the Pentagon Papers. However, my time was completely taken up with the implementation of the Cabinet Committee for International Narcotics Control.

In October 1971, Ehrlichman told me that the president wanted some advice regarding how best to deal with J. Edgar Hoover. We had not been pleased with the support we had received over the previous months from the FBI, and the president wanted better cooperation from Hoover. Because Liddy had had a career in the FBI, I asked him to prepare a memorandum on a potential request for a resignation from Hoover before the end of 1971. Liddy spent two weeks preparing the memo for me, dated October 22, 1971, entitled "Directorship of the FBI." I felt that this memo was as comprehensive, incisive, and persuasive a document as I had seen. It sketched out the history of the FBI, including its early successes, but also what happened when things started to deteriorate in the 1950s. Liddy recounted the current attacks against the FBI by the press, for example, by Maxine Cheshire in the *Washington Post*.

I forwarded this memo to Ehrlichman, who sent it on to the president. I learned that the president thought it was the best memorandum he had seen in years and wanted other memos to be modeled after it. Ehrlichman followed up with a call to Liddy and said, "Your memo on Hoover came back with A-pluses all over it." While the president, Ehrlichman, and I may have concluded that the FBI would be better off with Hoover gone, we did not have to do anything about it. On May 2, 1972, he died with his boots on.

The Fielding break-in on September 3, 1971, concluded the seven-week period that doomed Nixon's presidency, though that would not be clear for three more years. Nixon was first reelected by a landslide. But the moral authority of his administration had been terminally compromised. In those seven weeks, the SIU had undergone a journey from suspicion to certainty to covert action to frustration to zealotry: hardened by their first action, the Plumbers knew that the rules of engagement had been changed and the conventional respect for laws set aside. A botched break-in, evidenced in a few Polaroids, didn't seem to represent much. In practice, however, it was the first irreversible step by which a presidency ran out of control.

PART II

The Making of a True Believer

CHAPTER 6

Finding a Better Solution in Vietnam

My participation in the planning and execution of the criminal conspiracy can be understood more fully against the background of two seminal experiences, one in government, one that predated it. The deeply personal component of these experiences tied me closely to both Nixon the man, in perhaps one of his rawest hours of emotional openness, and Nixon the policymaker, a man who supported what I believed to be the key to solving the Vietnam War. My upbringing in a patriotic family had led me into the military and a belief in our government, while my experiences in Vietnam and with Nixon at the Lincoln Memorial led me to believe in Nixon himself and what he was trying to achieve.

My family was very patriotic, and loyalty to country and willingness to serve were instilled in me from my earliest years. After graduation from college, I enlisted in the Navy. During my short Navy career from December 1961 to June 1965, I served on the USS *Yorktown* (CVS 10) as a communications watch officer, radio and signals division officer, and officer of the deck underway. *Yorktown* was a famous World War II, Essex-class aircraft carrier.

She had been given the name "The Fighting Lady" because of her heroic battles from 1943 to 1945 in the Pacific Theater. (In the 1960s she was known by the more affectionate nickname, the *Yorkimaru*.) She had been converted from an attack carrier to an antisubmarine warfare ship because she was too small to handle the large jet fighters of the 1960s. When I served on her, the air wing consisted mostly of S2E Grumman propeller aircraft and Sikorsky helicopters used for dropping and monitoring submarine-detecting sonobuoys and also for guarding planes flying sorties during air operations.

Part of my job as a communications watch officer was to decode highly sensitive classified information. From 1965 to 1968, cryptography technology moved from the heavy typewriter machines, whose rotors had to be reprogrammed daily to decode five-letter group messages, to much more sophisticated on-line automatic cryptography. When we were in the western Pacific on "Westpac" cruises, most of the classified information that came into the communications department related to the movements and tactical operations of carrier task group (CTG) 70.4, the antisubmarine warfare group, of which the *Yorktown* was the flagship. While *Yorktown* officers and enlisted men were not informed about high policy questions, we were constantly admonished to keep classified any information about our ship's movements. In apparently flagrant breakdowns in security, female employees of the bars in Yokosuka and Sasebo, Japan, Hong Kong, and Subic Bay in the Philippines always knew when the *Yorktown* would arrive and depart. Regular warnings from officers that "loose lips sink ships" could not stop this.

CTG 70.4 operated primarily around Japan, Okinawa, the Philippines, and, in 1964 and 1965, off the coast of Vietnam. We had two lengthy at-sea cruises in and around Point Yankee, the moving locus of the U.S. naval fleet off the coast of Vietnam after the Gulf of Tonkin incident. Pounded into the minds of communications personnel, whether in the enlisted or officer ranks, was the paramount importance of maintaining the secrecy of the classified information we were handling. In fact, the understanding of the need for protecting classified information begins before joining a ship, when it is drilled into every officer candidate during training.

During my officer candidate school days in 1962, I learned right away that losing or misplacing my confidential operations manual was a serious offense. Like most of my fellow officer candidates, I kept a 24/7 mental check on its location. When I slept, it was locked up and I was the only one who had the combination to my locker. My time in OCS and on the *Yorktown* instilled in me the strongest commitment to protect the classified information entrusted to me.

After leaving the Navy, I received GI bill financial support and enrolled in law school as the Vietnam War was starting to ramp up. From 1965 to 1969, the war was a heavy backdrop to everything else happening in the country. Rare was the week at the University of Washington when there wasn't some kind of protest, march, speech, or sit-in decrying the U.S. war effort. During this period the number of U.S. military personnel assigned to the war increased to 530,000.

My personal view about the war began to change during my law school days. During my Navy stint, I had accepted the "domino theory" as an explanation for why the United States had to increase its efforts in Vietnam. That theory claimed that if communism was not stopped in Vietnam, it would spread to other countries in the region such as Laos, Cambodia, Thailand, and Malaysia. During law school, however, I began to feel that President Johnson's strategy was not working. Too much emphasis was being placed on purely military measures. As I began to see it, the Vietnam War was more of a civil struggle, and to win it we had to be much more aware of the underlying conditions in which the rural Vietnamese population lived and also more concerned with improving the lives of the average Vietnamese.

A research trip to South Vietnam with one of my law professors in December 1967 and January 1968 underscored my belief that a different approach would be necessary to end the war on acceptable terms. When Nixon ran for president in 1968, he campaigned hard on the need for a new plan to end the Vietnam War. He did not spell out the details of the plan, but in my view any plan would be better than the Johnson policies that were then grinding forward. Johnson's answer to every setback from the Vietcong or North Vietnamese main force units was to send more troops, drop more bombs, and conduct more search-and-destroy missions.

The research trip I took was short, but it vividly brought home to me the tragic reality of the war and contributed greatly to my belief in President Nixon's national security objectives in Vietnam. The trip was primarily designed to conduct research on an initiative that I felt was critical—a vastly expanded land-to-the-tiller land reform program. At that time I felt that a fully implemented policy of land reform could help end the war.

During my second year of law school in 1967, I had edited one of Professor Roy Prosterman's articles on land reform in South America for the *University of Washington Law Review*. In the course of that work I had become an ardent believer in his fundamental idea that if landless peasant farmers were given some type of ownership of the land they tilled, they would be much less likely to be converted by Communist propaganda to join the Vietcong insurgency. While the Communists promised to give land to landless peasants, their ultimate goal was not to establish a system of privately owned and farmed plots of land, but to form large-scale farm collectives. This had been the Communist strategy in both Russia and China. In contrast to the collectivist approach, effective non-Communist land reform involved vesting an ownership interest in the peasant and his family. Such ownership would result in peasant farmers investing more through "sweat equity" in the land they possessed, and economic progress would literally flow "from the ground up." The economic miracles in Japan, South Korea, and Taiwan were the results of effective land reform programs. I felt that by expanding land reform throughout South Vietnam, there was a chance that the United States and the South Vietnamese government could win the war against the Vietcong insurgency.

Just before I was to take my final exams at the end of the first quarter of my third year of law school, I asked Professor Prosterman how I could help him with his work on land reform. He told me that he was due to return to Vietnam in a few days and asked whether I would like to accompany him. This meant that I would have to cram three final exams into a day and a half, risk losing ground in my class standing, leave before the quarter ended on December 8, and miss Christmas with my wife and two-and-a-half-year-old son Peter. I told him that I wanted to go very much.

"Well, let me see what Bill Bredo, the head of our team at Stanford Research, thinks," Prosterman said. He dialed a number, then said, "Hi, Bill. Say, I've got a third-year law student here, and I'd like to bring him along on this next trip. There's a lot of material to wade through, he knows about land reform, and I think he can make a contribution." He listened for about half a minute, cupped his hand over the phone, and asked me, "Would a thousand dollars for four weeks' work be okay?" I nodded furiously (that was about $1,000 more than I expected to make over the Christmas holiday), mouthed, "Yes, sir!!" and gave him two thumbs up. Prosterman smiled at me and said, "He's up for it, Bill. Thanks so much. We'll see you in Saigon."

Our task was to prepare a report on the effectiveness of the laws and legal structures that were the foundation of the land reform efforts then under way in South Vietnam. Prosterman was a leading scholar on the legal aspects of land tenure systems in developing countries throughout the world. He had been serving as a principal consultant to the Stanford Research Institute, a firm that had been retained by the United States Agency for International Development (USAID) to conduct the overall study of the land reform program. My assignment was to translate and evaluate from the perspective of due process about one hundred cases decided by the four land reform courts in South Vietnam. This entailed meeting with top officials of the land reform commission to gain access to the cases and to collate and interpret them. With the help of a French-speaking Vietnamese translator, I was to translate the case texts from Vietnamese into French and then into English. My two years of college French was almost adequate preparation for this task. In particular, however, I felt that I needed to understand what was really happening in the Vietnamese countryside. And that's how I found myself leaving Saigon on Christmas Day 1967 in a bright red Buick.

We drove the Buick out of Saigon around 6:30 A.M. that day into the contested areas during a twenty-four-hour ceasefire. My companions were Elizabeth Pond, a college friend and the Saigon-based correspondent for the *Christian Science Monitor*; Dennis Blewitt, the Far East correspondent for the *London Daily Express*; our guide, Tran Ba Loc; and our worried, muttering driver.

Our car was so garish that we felt confident it could hardly be mistaken by the Vietcong for a military vehicle or one used by the CIA or USAID. The clasped-hands symbol of cooperation between the South Vietnamese and U.S. governments that was painted on the sides of the government-issue International Harvester Scouts was not the message we wanted to convey that day. We were looking for the enemy. Besides, we were dressed as tourists in sneakers, golf shirts, slacks, and sandals—there wasn't a hint of camouflage among the five of us. We looked instead like we were heading for the Jersey shore.

Our Vietnamese guide, Tran Ba Loc, was smaller than most Vietnamese men, with a wiry build and quick movements. He spoke English and French with jackhammer rapidity. Loc sat sideways in the front passenger seat and pointed out sites as we drove. Traffic on the roads of Saigon early Christmas morning was sparse. Only a few motorcycles snarled around us. This was a far cry from the night before. With the curfew lifted under the terms of the ceasefire, the streets had been filled on Christmas Eve with thousands of motorcycles and scooters revving their engines and charging everywhere. It was like one insane, collective joyride. A half-million riders and passengers bolted, dodged, and bucked through jammed streets with no place to go. They seemed to be always on the verge of a monumental pileup.

But by Christmas morning the din had dispersed and we drove through relatively quiet streets. Reminding us of the beauty and grace also present in that stricken land was the occasional sight of a young woman in her traditional long *ao dai* dress walking slowly along the side of the road, stepping gingerly around piles of junk and rocks.

The morning was already warm and humid, and the sun cast a pinkish glow on the eastern horizon. The air was choked with heavy gas fumes and the fetid smells of old vegetables and garbage. The nasty stench of *nuoc mam*, the pungent, fermented fish sauce that flavors most Vietnamese dishes, occasionally wafted through our open windows.

We were headed east out the Bien Hoa Highway, past the huge military base there, and then to Xuan Loc, the capital of

Long Khanh Province, about eighty kilometers northeast of Saigon. Somewhere on our journey that day, Elizabeth and Dennis hoped to find a representative of the National Liberation Front (the "Vietcong") for an interview on the conditions they would need for settlement of the war. They felt that with the Christmas ceasefire in place, they would have a better chance of locating a Vietcong cadre who would talk with them. My goals for the trip were to learn as much as possible about conditions in the countryside outside of Saigon, to gain knowledge that I hoped would inform my work on land reform, and mostly to be able to feel the rhythms of life in the predominantly rural areas of South Vietnam.

The three bridges that crossed rivers out to the Bien Hoa base were heavily fortified. Sandbagged bunkers guarded the four corners of each bridge. U.S. military vehicles streamed everywhere. As we approached the huge military base, we saw heavily sandbagged Army checkpoints at all entrances and soldiers with M–16s and machine guns looking out of metal turrets. The Long Binh base in the south, which was close to Bien Hoa, and Cam Ranh Bay in the north were the principal bases for soldiers arriving in and leaving South Vietnam, which explained the busy traffic.

Past the Bien Hoa base, we drove into a new world, a vast rubber plantation. Long rows of rubber trees fingered out from the highway in perfect horizontal lines. There was no undergrowth. A six-inch carpet of green grass beneath the trees looked to be constantly trimmed. As we drove through the plantation, Loc told us about Vietcong mines. He said they were normally placed along the sides of the road. The targets were U.S. vehicles. He told us about one hapless civilian Vietnamese driver who ran over a mine that killed his two civilian passengers. The Vietcong fined the driver 20,000 piasters, almost a month's income. This covered the cost of the mine, which had to be leg-carried from North Vietnam, and served as a warning to the driver to stay in the middle of the road. I checked to make sure our unhappy driver was keeping the middle of the road directly under the middle of our Buick.

Suddenly Loc told the driver to pull over quickly to the right of the road. We came to a stop, and Loc jumped out. He had seen two peasant women wearing coolie hats picking rubber from the bowls on the trees. He wanted to interview them. I had been thinking about mines. We all got out and joined him. He asked if there were any Vietcong close by. One of the women said that a month before some bombs had been dropped very nearby. Loc told us in French that the woman had referred to the Vietcong as "les frères de l'autre côte"—the brothers of the other side. She said she worked every day except Tet for ninety piasters (about seventy-six cents) a day plus rice. We learned that we were on the d'Ong Que plantation. The other woman added nothing, so we retreated to the car.

As we drove off, Loc told us that French holding companies still dominated rubber growing in South Vietnam. They might have lost the war at Dien Bien Phu in 1954, but they had not lost the economic battle for rubber. One unintended consequence of America fighting the war, I thought to myself, was to keep Vietnam safe for the French rubber industry. Later that day we met a young French couple living securely in what to all Americans was a very dangerous area. Loc said that the French paid their taxes to the Vietcong like everyone else, and once they paid they were left alone.

We passed a U.S. Army tank unit, and I knew there would be no turkey for those boys today. Many of them had their shirts off and were sunning themselves. The tanks were positioned at four corners of a small rectangle just off the left of the road. To the right, a Vietnamese regional force unit was encamped surrounded by heavy bunkers. We passed large fields of banana trees that Loc called the "Prairie of Banana Trees." He said that another name for the area was "Ambush Alley." Our driver was getting increasingly worried and muttered more loudly. He constantly looked over his shoulder. He told Loc in high-pitched Vietnamese that if he had known where we wanted him to drive us today, he would never have done it. I did not blame him.

We crossed what we learned later was the abandoned Susannah rubber plantation. Loc told us that he expected to introduce us as Eastern European press if we made contact with the Vietcong. For some weird reason, he said that I reminded him of an Italian. Maybe he had met some Italians who were six feet tall, fairly solid, with strong Scandinavian features. The only thing about me that could be remotely perceived as Italian were my leather sandals. I was certainly not carrying a map or anything that would identify me as an American. I had left all identification in Saigon and carried only piasters, the local currency dating from French colonial times. Carrying no identification at all was suspicious, but it seemed suicidal to carry a reserve officer's identification card, a student card issued by the Associated Students of the University of Washington, or a Washington State driver's license.

Leaving the rubber and banana tree areas, we headed east and drove through several more small villages. When we stopped for a short break about thirty kilometers east of Bien Hoa, we heard the *whop-whop-whop* of U.S. helicopters flying high overhead. Elizabeth said that they were monitoring the use of Highway 1 because one of the conditions of the Christmas ceasefire was that no military movements were to occur during that day. It seemed obvious to me that this condition wouldn't be a hardship for the Vietcong, because they seldom risked the exposure of using a major highway like Highway 1 anyway. Most Vietcong movement, I had been told, occurred at night and along small rural roads and trails.

After three hours, we drove into the town of Xuan Loc, the capital of Long Khanh Province. We learned that Xuan Loc was a predominantly Catholic city, and a large cathedral dominated the center of the town. Loc told us that the priests, mostly Vietnamese, who went south in 1954 set up the parishes and were very powerful in southern Vietnamese society. We drove through to the east side of Xuan Loc, made a sharp left turn, and stopped in front of a one-story white building, the provincial hospital of Long Khanh, the Benh Vien Xuan Loc. The hospital was the first place Elizabeth wanted to visit because she felt that this was where we would best understand the tragic effect of the war on innocent civilians.

A tall, soft-faced nurse greeted us at the entrance and took us into the war casualty ward. We saw Vietnamese civilians with missing feet and arms and with holes in their bodies who had been innocent victims of cross fires, strafing attacks, and mortar and mine explosions. An old man, wearing black, stood next to the bed of one of his daughters. His other daughter was in the next bed. Both girls, about fifteen and seventeen, were asleep or in a coma. Other beds contained one, two, sometimes three people. Whole families were here, caring for the hurt ones. A man, his face contorted by grief, perched on a bed where a little boy was lying. He pulled up the boy's right pajama leg to reveal a flat stub wrapped in bandages. He told Loc that the little boy was a victim of a Vietcong grenade. I looked more closely at the man and saw that he had no left leg—it had been amputated about seven inches below the groin. Loc had introduced us as members of the press. A few patients smiled at us. Most of them just stared fixedly at us.

We left the ward and went to the quarters and dining area of the Filipino medical team that operated the hospital. We were surprised to see two Americans, one a doctor, the other a medic, attached to the Eleventh Armored Cavalry Regiment. The American doctor occasionally came to the hospital to help with difficult operations. He spoke bitterly about the ward and detested the killing. The chief of the Filipino team, a Dr. Zeniga, answered our questions. He told us that when there were military campaigns in the area, up to twenty Vietnamese civilians would require attention. Because of the heavy dust, rains, and lack of sanitation, resistance to disease was very low. War wounds were suffered from both Vietcong and friendly fire. His team treated wounded Vietcong when they were brought in by the police. When the teams went into the villages of the province, they treated the Vietcong who came in as civilians. A doctor and nurse from the teams were always out in the villages. Loc asked if the teams had ever been ambushed. "Oh, yes," he replied unconcernedly. He marked two spots on a wall map where the teams had been attacked. Loc asked if they went out armed. "Oh, no. Never," he replied.

Outside the hospital we spoke to the father of one of the children we had visited. He gave us his name—Phan Van Xinh—and told us that he was a farmer. He told us that the day before his young son and some friends had mistakenly wandered into a zone that was off-limits to everyone. A U.S. helicopter, mistaking the children for a Vietcong cadre, had strafed them. The doctors had just operated on Phan's twelve-year-old son, amputating a leg and an arm. The other children had suffered less serious wounds. Phan told us that his son would recover. I took a picture of Phan that I have kept for forty years. I keep it to remind myself of the terrible toll of war on innocent civilians—and especially children—which came home with searing clarity during our hospital visit.

After our visit to the hospital, we headed back toward Saigon, looking for a place where we might have an opportunity to meet the Vietcong. Approximately sixteen kilometers southwest of Xuan Loc, we came upon a group of people milling about in the road who seemed highly agitated. We stopped our car, and when we got out a young man came running up to us holding a spent bullet in his hand. To Loc's question as to what had happened, the young man told us that an Army helicopter had flown in low over the treetops and fired machine-gun rounds along the road. He took us over to a tree and showed us a lower limb that had been shattered, he said, by the bullet he was holding. Loc asked the young man why he thought the Americans had fired during the ceasefire, and he said that it might have been because the Vietcong were transporting wounded cadre along the road. When I asked him if I could see the spent bullet, he gave it to me.

Loc said that if this place had just been strafed, it was probable that there were some Vietcong in the vicinity. He suggested that we get off Highway 1 and head back into the field to the north.

We walked into the field for about half a mile, skirted a rubber plantation, and then stopped at a lean-to shelter that appeared to be a place for peasant farmers to rest. We took out the fruit and water we had carried with us and ate lunch. Loc wandered off into the bush and returned about a half-hour later. He said that he had seen no one and that this was probably not a good place to find the Vietcong. He said that the area was too wide open and did not provide good cover. We waited a few more minutes and then headed back to our car. To any curious cadre who may have been watching, we were just a few crazy Westerners off for a picnic.

When we got back to Highway 1, we were feeling that it was unlikely we would meet with any Vietcong that day. It was getting on toward midafternoon, and we wanted to get back to

Saigon well before dark. We drove about fifteen more kilometers, and then Loc told the driver to stop at a small hamlet on the north side of the road. We got out of the car, and as we started to walk into the hamlet several small children ran toward us yelling. I thought I saw one child hold up his forefinger and middle finger in a "V" and point to his eyes. This, I had been told, was a common signal among soldiers to indicate the presence of the Vietcong, or "VC." But why, I wondered, would a Vietnamese child know it? I couldn't understand what they were saying, but Loc increased his pace and pointed to a man in shorts and a round canvas, expeditionary military hat who, on seeing us, started walking very fast out the back of the hamlet while flogging an ox that he was leading away. The man was wearing a holstered sidearm. Elizabeth, Dennis, and I jogged to keep up with Loc, who was now running after the man. When we reached the other side of the hamlet, Loc came back and told us to wait for him. He pointed to a small clearing with a few fallen logs surrounded by high grass and told us to wait there until he returned. We sat down and waited.

At this point in our day, I was beginning to doubt the soundness of our decision to venture off the main road. We had been told by many people that this area just northeast of Saigon was pretty secure, but if Loc was successful in locating a Vietcong cadre this close to Highway 1, what did that say about security here or elsewhere? When I asked Elizabeth what she thought, she said that Loc was very adept and capable. He would not lead us into a dangerous situation. Time stretched out slowly.

"What do you think?" I asked again about forty-five minutes later. "He'll be back soon," she replied. After another twenty minutes, we heard some swishing in the tall grass, and then Loc emerged grinning. He was almost panting, and we could tell that he had been running for a while. He told us that he had made contact with a midlevel Vietcong cadre, and that this man had agreed to an interview with Elizabeth and Dennis. However, he said, the interview would not take place that day but a week later, on New Year's Day. He pointed to me and said, "But you can't come because you're CIA." So now I knew what the Vietcong thought about me. He said that he had been told where he, Elizabeth, and Dennis would meet the cadre next week, but that he would not be able to tell us beforehand.

Elizabeth and Dennis were very excited that they had been able to make contact, and as we walked back to our car they were already making plans for that day. She told me that she was disappointed that I would not be able to come. But she said that it would help her if I would tell Barry Zorthian, the head of the Joint United States Public Affairs Office (JUSPAO), where she was going on New Year's Day in case she didn't return. Loc told her that the name of the hamlet where the interview was to occur was Tra Co. I told them that this information would be of little help if she was captured or killed.

When we rolled into Saigon that night, I felt relieved. I had been struck by how relatively easy it had been for Loc to find a Vietcong cadre so close to Saigon. Little did I know that the specific area where Loc had located the Vietcong cadre was a principal staging area for a battalion-size unit of the Vietcong. That same unit later attacked Bien Hoa and then broke through to attack Saigon during the Tet offensive on January 31, 1968.

In reflecting on what we had seen that day, I understood that while it looked to us as if we were in a safe, secure area, we were actually in the heart of enemy country. Any number of things could have resulted in tragedy, from being strafed by American helicopters to getting blown up by Vietcong mines. The peasant woman Loc interviewed in the first rubber plantation we drove through had described the Vietcong as "the brothers of the other side." If she was a typical peasant in seeing the Vietcong as brothers, there was a long way to go to convince them that the Vietcong were enemies to be defeated by the government of South Vietnam and American forces. Seeing Vietnamese men, women, and children who had suffered horrible wounds from both U.S. and Vietcong forces—the "collateral damage," in military jargon—was compelling evidence of the personal pain caused by the conflict.

The Christmas Day trip brought home to me more than anything else how precarious the U.S. position was in South Vietnam. It was the foundation for my belief that we had to find a better way to extricate ourselves from that war. Ending the Vietnam War on terms that could bring lasting peace was the deep-seated goal that would drive much of my thinking and work over the next few years.

Over the next week and a half following our Christmas Day journey, I completed my portion of the report for Roy Prosterman's overall assessment of the status of South Vietnam land reform. My focus was on how fairly the court system treated the tenant farmers who had grievances. Le Van Toan, the commissioner general for land reform, spent hours with me explaining how the four land reform courts in the provinces of An Giang, Long An, Dinh Tuong, and Saigon actually functioned. Counsel was usually provided by the government to the tenants, while landlords usually retained their own lawyers. Toan indicated that he felt this was a fair system.

Toward the end of our four weeks in Vietnam, Prosterman completed development of a new land reform proposal for South Vietnam. We agreed that on our return to the United States we would make a substantial effort to advocate in the U.S. media and in Congress for a new policy shift in support of the proposal. But before flying back, there remained one assignment that I had taken on during my Christmas Day trip with Elizabeth Pond and Dennis Blewitt.

On January 1 in Saigon, I set up shop in the Caravelle Hotel, where Dennis Blewitt had a room. Early that morning, Dennis, Elizabeth, and Loc had driven out to the contested area during the New Year's Day ceasefire for their prearranged interview with the Vietcong cadre. I was exceedingly anxious about them, and my restlessness made it difficult to work on my report. As the afternoon passed into evening and dusk settled over Saigon, I was getting ready to go over to JUSPAO and report in to Barry Zorthian. Just before I left, the three of them knocked on my door at the Caravelle. I was very glad and relieved to see them. Both of them were thrilled that they had made contact with the Vietcong, and we celebrated with a magnificent dinner at a restaurant on the outskirts of Saigon with Beverly Deepe, another reporter and a colleague of Elizabeth's. Toward the end of the evening, Dennis and Elizabeth were anxious to get to their typewriters to begin writing their stories. They had scored a major scoop, and there was no time to lose in getting their reports written and published.

Before leaving Saigon, I was also able to provide Elizabeth with copious notes and background information that Prosterman and I had accumulated on land reform. Our hope was that she would see the land reform proposal as serious and that, with her keen analytical ability, she would be able to write thorough and balanced articles on the subject in the future. Her measured and evenhanded reporting on land reform over the next few months surpassed our fondest hopes.

During a meeting with Congressman Paul N. "Pete" McCloskey later in the trip, I learned much more about the problems of the counter-insurgency effort in which the United States was engaged. McCloskey had just won a surprising victory in a

California congressional district race against Shirley Temple Black. During his campaign he had expressed strong doubts about the war. Right after winning, he took a trip to Saigon to get a firsthand look at how the war was being waged. He and John Ehrlichman had been good friends during law school at Stanford University, and Ehrlichman had urged me to look up McCloskey if he showed up in Saigon while I was there.

Through the media grapevine, I found out that McCloskey was staying at the Caravelle Hotel. I went to meet him with the idea that I might get a chance to brief him on Prosterman's land reform ideas. When I walked into his room, I found a man of great charisma and manic energy. With his square jaw, short, thick dark hair, and Clint Eastwood squint, Pete McCloskey looked like the ideal marine. But he did not just look the part; he was the real deal. For valor and wounds suffered in combat during the Korean War, McCloskey had been awarded the Navy Cross, the Silver Star, and two Purple Hearts.

He welcomed me to his room, where he was simultaneously toweling off from a quick shower, jumping into clean undershorts, talking on the phone, and getting ready for dinner with friends. He had just returned from a visit with his former unit, the Fifth Marine Regiment, which had given him an unvarnished report about the war, marine to marine. What he learned had not pleased him. He said that our military tactics often resulted in the destruction of rural hamlets and that this was creating more enemies for us. I told him that was my impression as well. Although I had only an hour to meet with him, I was able to give him a brief overview of the land reform work that Prosterman and I were doing. McCloskey immediately grasped the value of land reform to the overall war effort, and he became a dedicated supporter of our program during his early years in Congress from 1967 to 1974.

From that meeting in Saigon until today, Pete McCloskey has been a close friend. Once he likes you, he will do anything for you. While his physical courage was repeatedly demonstrated in wartime, his moral courage and kindness was fully displayed in the aftermath of the Watergate tragedy.

I returned to the United States and Seattle on January 4, 1968. It was wonderful to see my wife Suzanne and son Peter again. I told them and other family members and many groups of friends about what I had seen and learned during the trip. Particularly gratifying right after our return was the January 5, 1968, edition of the *Christian Science Monitor*, which contained a lengthy story on Vietnam land reform by Elizabeth Pond. She criticized the current program and concluded with a description of the new land reform program advocated by Roy Prosterman. The U.S. share of that program was a projected cost of $450 million—or the cost of one week's worth of fighting the war. She concluded her article with Prosterman's observation that if a successful new land reform program could win enough support from the rural peasants to shorten the war by only one week, it would have paid for itself. Prosterman and I were extremely pleased with this coverage, and we spread the article around as widely as we could. Three weeks later a stunning attack gave greater urgency to our cause.

Suzanne and I were sitting in the living room in our little house in Seattle three miles from the University of Washington campus watching the evening news on January 30, 1968. News stories throughout the day had been saturated with details of the offensive launched by the Vietcong at multiple targets throughout South Vietnam at the beginning of the Tet holiday. My attention was riveted on where the attacks had been mounted. Suddenly I leaned forward to get closer to the television so that I could better see what was being shown. To my shock, a television cameraman had positioned himself so that he could successfully film the launch of a rocket by a Vietcong cadre operating from an unfinished office building that I recognized—it was located approximately two hundred feet from the hotel where Prosterman and I regularly ate our lunch on a fifth-floor balcony. We had gazed daily at this unfinished building, and its shape and contour were etched in my memory. This building (and our hotel) were located a short distance from the palace grounds where the rocket had been aimed and, I learned later, been detonated. "Can you believe that, Suzanne? The VC are attacking in the heart of Saigon. I was right there. They must have been right in the city planning the best places to attack for the past several weeks. I wonder if some of them worked in our hotel. No place is safe in that country."

History records that the Tet offensive unleashed by the Vietcong on January 30, 1968, had been planned for several months. The Tet offensive has been described as a crushing military defeat for the Communist forces. According to one account, while it was apparent that neither the Vietcong nor the North Vietnamese Army had achieved any of their tactical goals, the simple fact that they could mount such a large-scale and deadly attack gave the Vietcong a huge psychological and propaganda victory. From this point forward, U.S. public support for the Vietnam War deteriorated and opposition become increasingly intense.

Over the next few weeks, Prosterman and I traveled around America, advocating for land reform in Vietnam. We went to the East Coast on a lobbying mission in early March 1968. I went to Boston to explain the new land reform program to editors at the *Christian Science Monitor*. Prosterman went to New York City to brief the *New York Times*. We joined up in Washington, D.C., to brief congressional experts, particularly congressmen John Moss (D-Calif.) and Ogden Reid (R-N.Y.), who were both indefatigable supporters of a workable Vietnam land reform program. Senator Warren Magnuson (D-Wash.) and his chief of staff, Gerald Grinstein, also became avid proponents of our new program. But even with strong support from major Democratic leaders in Congress, we were not receiving any effective support from the U.S. State Department. The report that Prosterman prepared for the Government Operations Committee, chaired by Congressman Moss, stated: "The failure to undertake a sweeping and genuine land reform in South Vietnam assuredly is costing, during each year of delay, the lives of large numbers of American soldiers over and above the number that would otherwise be killed. It is significantly prolonging the war."

Prosterman's report became the foundation for our individual briefings over the next few weeks. We felt that we had to try to persuade the Johnson administration to change its course and come out for the kind of widespread, major land reform program that could have a positive effect in the countryside.

In late March 1968, I participated in a panel at the University of Washington that focused on the current conditions in South Vietnam. I pointed out to the audience the dangers of drawing broad conclusions from the anecdotes I was recounting from my recent trip. With that caveat, I shared some candid opinions. My message was that primary reliance by the Johnson administration on military solutions constituted a failure to understand the revolutionary struggle that was going on in Vietnam. I said that winning the "hearts and minds" of the rural peasantry, a political process, had to become the central goal of U.S. policy. The major focus therefore needed to be political, not military. By political I meant doing everything feasible to gain and not lose the active support of the rural population for the South Vietnamese government. This meant that even in military conflicts with U.S. troops, an enlightened, tough commander would be willing to risk increased casualties to achieve the right psychological and political effect rather than hold down casualties to get a high enemy body count but the wrong effect. It meant rescinding the apparent standing order for pilots of American helicopters to fire indiscriminately on villages that fired on them as they flew over. This order had risked the loss of too many innocent civilian lives. It meant ending the regular tactic of "search and destroy," which had resulted in ripping up rural areas when U.S. troops were fighting the Vietcong and North Vietnamese main force units but leaving nothing stable and secure afterwards.

I acknowledged that many South Vietnamese had been helped tremendously by the generous efforts of U.S. military personnel in pacification programs and that many USAID programs had improved the quality of life in the countryside. However, I concluded, not nearly enough had been done to solve the root problems, which were caused by the contradictions and disparities of South Vietnamese life and included the gaps between the rich and the poor, the landed and the landless, Catholic and Buddhist, Conchinchinese and Tonkinese, youth and elders, factions and secret societies, government and revolution. These types of conflicts appear in many underdeveloped countries, but in South Vietnam they provided the grist for the insurgency mill, and thousands of our soldiers were dying as a result. We simply were not using the available tools—such as a massive land reform program—to attempt to solve at least one of the principal gaps: the great divide between the landowning classes and the landless rural peasantry.

My trip to Vietnam helped me understand how critical it was to develop and implement good policy if we were to have any chance of achieving our goals and purposes.

Later, when I was working on the White House staff, I was able to introduce Roy Prosterman to Dick Smyser, the National

Security Council staff member who advised Dr. Henry Kissinger on Vietnam policy. Smyser became a believer in land reform, and he was able to persuade Kissinger of its importance.

It was very gratifying to me to see President Nixon establish land reform as one of the major efforts the South Vietnamese government had to undertake. In a meeting with President Thieu at Midway in the spring of 1969, President Nixon expressed special interest in Thieu's new concepts of land distribution—based in part on Roy Prosterman's proposal—and offered American cooperation to bring it about. Nixon's support for land reform, his plan to gradually withdraw U.S. troops from the war, and his support for "Vietnamization," a program to shift the burden of the fight to the South Vietnamese Army, were all elements, I believed, of a sound Vietnam policy. The Vietnam trip and the following events cemented my belief that the president's war policy was "the only game in town."

My trip to Vietnam was more than just an exercise in developing land reform as an important policy initiative. It was also a deeply emotional experience that drove me to seek ways to participate, in however small a way, in changing the course of the war. That I would take a month out of my third year of law school to go to Vietnam, immerse myself in policy work, drive through dangerous areas during a putative "ceasefire," and then travel the United States to advocate for a different approach were extreme measures driven by my passionate belief in finding a better solution in Vietnam. My later commitment to President Nixon's plans for ending the Vietnam War was based in part on his support for Roy Prosterman's land reform ideas. Major land reform measures were in fact instituted in South Vietnam in 1970 and 1971 by President Thieu, in response to Nixon's support.

CHAPTER 7

Nixon at the
Lincoln Memorial

Although Richard Nixon was important to me as an authority figure, I became much closer to him personally when I followed him during one of the most moving, bizarre, and potentially dangerous ventures of his presidency. For the first time, I observed him in a crisis mode digging deep into his reservoirs of intellect and emotion. What I saw him say and do that day affected me strongly and bound me more closely to him than ever before. The episode began with an alarming message from a Secret Service agent.

"Searchlight is on the lawn!" I looked up in shock as these tense words about the location of "Searchlight," President Nixon's Secret Service code name, crackled over the loudspeaker in the Service's command post in the Old Executive Office Building. It was 4:15 A.M. on May 9, 1970. A few hours before, in the evening of May 8, the president had explained in a news conference why he had ordered a military "incursion" into Cambodia. His comments had added fuel to the firestorm of frustration and rage among tens of thousands of students and other antiwar activists around the country. Those activists and students who lived closest to the District of Columbia were headed directly to the capital to vent their anger and grief. We had good reason to fear a violent and possibly lethal confrontation.

The president's news conference the night of May 8 followed the tragedy at Kent State University in Ohio just a few days before on May 4. The Kent State protest, like others on campuses throughout the country, was organized after news of the president's decision to attack Cambodia first became public knowledge on April 29. At Kent State, Governor John Rhodes had called up the National Guard to help maintain order on the campus. When the inevitable clash occurred, young, frightened National Guardsmen, who had been issued live ammunition, fired on a rock-throwing group of angry students, killing four of them. The picture of one girl kneeling next to the bodies and looking up in shock and anguish had already been widely reprinted, searing the minds of millions around the country. The Kent State killings were a painful and forceful reminder to me not to allow our government defenders to overreact and precipitate a worse tragedy. In *The Haldeman Diaries*, former chief of staff Bob Haldeman noted that when Nixon heard the news about the Kent State killings on May 4, he was "very disturbed." He was "afraid his decision set it off." Haldeman and the president talked that day about how they could get through to the students but came up with no plan.

I had just come into the command post to ensure that preparations to fortify the EOB and the White House were completed in preparation for the potentially violent protest that was brewing outside. Right after the first Secret Service announcement that "Searchlight is on the lawn" came a second: "Searchlight has asked for a car." These two announcements made no sense to me and sounded extremely ominous. The president was supposed to be asleep in the White House residence. All of our security precautions were predicated on keeping him safe within the White House grounds. Not once in our crisis management group meetings did anyone envision the possibility that the president would venture out on his own during this volatile, potentially incendiary day. Certainly not two hours before dawn.

Right at the start of the Nixon administration, John Ehrlichman had assigned me White House responsibility for participating in the crisis management group in the Department of Justice. Deputy Attorney General Dick Kleindienst chaired this group, and we would meet in his conference room whenever major antiwar demonstrations were planned. Antiwar demonstrations had been growing in intensity during the later years of the Johnson administration and the first year and a half of the Nixon administration. On day one of the Nixon administration over half a million U.S. military personnel were engaged in some way in Vietnam, and even more Americans were ready to demonstrate against the war throughout the country.

My first assignment as part of this group had been to monitor the measures that the government would take to oversee the counter-inaugural demonstration on January 20, 1969. The group had agreed that a permit should be granted to the protest group so that they could demonstrate within two blocks of the inaugural parade. Unfortunately, several demonstrators pushed outside their permitted area and were able to get within a few feet of the parade. My memo to Ehrlichman describing in detail how the government had responded to the protests eventually was routed to the president. In his own handwriting, he had questioned the advisability of granting a permit but concluded that on balance everyone had done a good job.

Later in 1969, I was heavily involved in planning the government's response to a major October demonstration called the "Moratorium Against the Vietnam War" and then a November demonstration organized by the New Mobilization Against the War in Vietnam. The "Mobe" brought over 300,000 demonstrators into the District of Columbia. In our planning meetings, I consistently urged active cooperation between the government and the demonstration organizers. It was clear to me that they had a constitutional right to come to the capital to express their grievances and that we in the government had a duty to help them do so without injury to them, to us, or to the city.

When the Moratorium organizers told us that they did not have the means to communicate with their own security monitors, our crisis management group agreed to let them use Secret Service walkie-talkies with crystals that would enable the crisis group to listen in. We wanted to know where their demonstration was headed so that we could provide backup security in case some protesters got out of control. The organizers agreed to this.

On a personal level, I knew many people, former schoolmates and teachers, who came to Washington, D.C., to protest the president's Vietnam War policy, and I did not want to risk taking actions that might hurt them. By the time of the Cambodia incursion and the firestorm of protests that ensued, the crisis management group was a tried and tested group that functioned well together.

As the president's deputy counsel with responsibility for monitoring overall security measures during times of physical threat to the White House, I had just completed my rounds to check on the military unit that was encamped in full combat gear on the fourth floor of the EOB. The troops had finished moving in and were lying down on the floor, some stretched out in their sleeping bags and some sitting on the floor leaning against the walls. After a movement that had taken most of the night, they looked exhausted. I had also confirmed that additional units of the Metropolitan Police Department would be available if needed. Earlier I had walked the perimeter of the White House defenses to ensure that the two hundred–plus buses we had leased on an emergency basis from local transit authorities formed a tight, continuous barricade just outside the White House fence. By 3:00 A.M., the last of the buses had been driven in and backed into position.

Buses surrounded the White House because I had persuaded the attorney general and the crisis management team that the White House would be better protected by a circle of buses than by several hundred police with helmets and clubs standing shoulder to shoulder. I told the team, "John Wayne had it right. He just circled the wagons when under attack!" I added that with buses as our first line of defense, protesters could break windows, paint graffiti, or punch holes in the tires. But they wouldn't be attacking people. If they tried to climb over the buses, we could squirt some tear gas to keep them back. Buses were not, I argued, as inherently threatening and provocative as a cordon of police officers in riot gear would be. After much discussion in which the idea was strongly supported by my friend Lieutenant General Bill McCaffrey, the senior military officer present and commander of the D.C. Army contingent, the crisis group finally bought in to this logic. The purpose of these extraordinary security measures was to keep over 100,000 angry protesters from storming the White House.

Right after the second announcement that the president had called for a car, I phoned the White House signal operator and asked him to ring John Ehrlichman immediately. When John answered and mumbled, "What's up?" I told him that the president was at large and had called for a car. "Go over to the lawn and see if you can render assistance." "Yes, sir!" I answered and then warned the Secret Service duty officer that I was going to be moving at speed over to the West Wing. I ran across West

Executive Drive, sprinted past the White House police desk inside the ground-floor West Wing entrance, took the steps two at a time up to the first floor, and arrived at the Rose Garden lawn just in time to see the president's limousine disappear out the south entrance next to the Northwest Gate.

After checking quickly with the Secret Service agent on duty, I learned that the president was heading to the Lincoln Memorial. I called Ehrlichman to let him know the president's destination and then immediately called for a car and directed the driver to take me there. After a high-speed ride, we arrived at the Memorial about four minutes later and stopped right behind the president's limousine, which was idling against the curb on the street between the Reflecting Pool and the Memorial. I ran up the steps but then slowed down when I saw the president talking with a group of students just inside the Memorial to the front and right of the famous statue of a brooding Lincoln sitting in a chair. It was still dark.

President Nixon was talking earnestly to about eight or ten students who had formed a loose circle around him. Manolo Sanchez, Nixon's valet, and Dr. Tkach, the physician who usually accompanied the president, were standing off to the side. Dr. Tkach looked tired and very worried. Other students were gradually moving over to join the circle when they realized who was there. Most disturbing, I counted only four Secret Service agents in the president's detail—a frighteningly small number for such a potentially dangerous situation. They were positioned around him so that they could maintain a 360-degree observation. I could tell from their faces that they were as fearful as I was. As Nixon wrote later, "I have never seen the Secret Service quite so petrified with apprehension." He certainly got that right.

From the back of the circle of students, I leaned in closer to observe the president and hear what he was saying. As I wrote later that day, "It appeared that he was trying very hard to reach out and into the students, to communicate with them. . . . He did carry the conversation for the most part . . . but this was necessary as the students themselves had hardly anything to say, and were too stunned to respond at all. His manner was reminiscent of the campaign where he would go into a group of people, shake hands and comment on those things which popped into his mind."

And a lot popped into his mind. The vast range and mastery of the subjects he discussed was monumental. That he could offer these ideas around 5:00 A.M. after just an hour of sleep made it an even greater tour de force of intellect, compassion, and focus. Although I could not hear every word he spoke, I was awed and moved by what I did hear. All of my previous meetings with the president had been somewhat formal briefings in the Oval Office or the Cabinet Room. This was the first time I had heard the president speak extemporaneously and straight from the heart.

In a memo Nixon dictated on May 13 about "what actually took place at the Lincoln Memorial," he expressed frustration that neither Ron Zeigler (who didn't join our traveling group until we were just leaving the Capitol) nor I got a clear understanding of what he was trying to communicate. He felt that we were too focused on the practical aspects of the visit—when he got up, how he looked in reaching out to the students, what he had for breakfast—than what was really important. He wrote that his staff "are enormously interested in material things, what we accomplish in our record . . . [but] very few seem to have any interest and, therefore, have no ability to communicate on those matters that are infinitely more important—qualities of spirit, emotion, of the depth and mystery of life which this whole visit really was all about."

The important thing was to communicate deeply significant ideas about our country, its problems, and their lives to students who might never have a chance to see and hear a president again. He told the students that his favorite spot in Washington was right there—the Lincoln Memorial at night.

He then asked if any of them had seen his press conference. Because most of them had been traveling the night before to get to D.C. to protest against him, only a few hands went up. He said that he was sorry they had missed it because he had explained during the conference that his "goals in Vietnam were the same as theirs—to stop the killing and end the war to bring peace. Our goal was not to get into Cambodia by what we were doing but to get out of Vietnam."

There was no response to this point, so he tried to find common ground with them by showing that he understood how they felt about the war. He said, "I know that probably most of you think I'm an SOB, but I want you to know that I understand just how you feel." He recounted his own antiwar views just before World War II. He said that because of his Quaker background, he had been as close to a pacifist as anybody could be in those times. He thought then that Neville Chamberlain, the British prime minister, was the "greatest man alive" when he came back from his negotiations with Hitler in Munich and announced that he had achieved "peace in our time." He had thought that Churchill was a "madman," but, he told the students, he later changed his mind. He said that while Chamberlain was a good man, Churchill was a wiser man, "because Churchill had not only the wisdom but the courage to carry out policies that he believed were right, even though there was a time when both in England and all over the world he was extremely unpopular because of his 'anti-peace' stand."

He expressed his understanding of why the race question was a major subject of concern on their campuses, and on the subject of America's terrible treatment of the American Indian, he said that "we had taken a proud and independent race and virtually destroyed them, and that we had to find ways to bring them back into decent lives in this country."

Nixon then told them how important it was to learn by traveling the country and the world. The students did not respond to this topic, so he moved on to the actions the government was taking to improve the environment by taking government property and putting it to better use than just military or other purposes. He gave a preview of his future China initiative by sharing his "great hopes that during my administration, and certainly during their lifetime, the great mainland of China would be opened up so that we could know the 700 million people who live in China, who are one of the most remarkable people on earth." He moved on to a discussion of Moscow, a "gray" place, and suggested that they visit Leningrad to really get to know Russia.

Following this travelogue, one of the students brought him back to why they were in Washington, D.C.: "I hope you realize that we are willing to die for what we believe in." Nixon answered, "I certainly realize that." He then discussed his environmental initiatives—cleaning up the air and water—and said that they were material problems that needed to be solved. However, he said with some passion, while we must make the country more beautiful and remove the "ugly blotches," we all needed to think about why we were really here. What were those elements of spirit that really mattered? He concluded by saying that he "just wanted to be sure that all of them realized that ending the war and cleaning up the streets and the air and the water was not going to solve spiritual hunger, which all of us have and which, of course, has been the great mystery of life from the beginning of time."

After these remarks, Manolo Sanchez pushed forward to tell the president that he had a call in the car. Sanchez, the agents, and I had noticed that more and more students were joining the group. I wrote later, "I turned around and looked out from the Memorial and saw that the Washington Monument was picking up a soft shade of pink. There was a haziness about the morning, and the profound quiet of the Lincoln Memorial blended beautifully with the changing morning colors." A surreal effulgence surrounded us. But the reality of an increasing number of protesting students heading toward us was ominous.

After more urging from Sanchez, the president finally agreed that it was time to go, shook a few hands, and then headed down the steps to his car. Before getting in, Dr. Tkach took a picture of the president with a man who said he was from Detroit. When the president, Dr. Tkach, and Sanchez drove away in the limousine, I jumped in my car and directed the driver to follow close behind.

My feelings at that point combined enormous relief that the president had not been harmed and a sense of amazement and awe that I had just witnessed one of history's most extraordinary presidential visits. I settled back in my seat assuming that we would head back to the White House. But the president's car did not take the left turn on Seventeenth Avenue but continued at speed on up Constitution Avenue toward the Capitol. What, I wondered, would happen next? I noticed out the window that the Mall was filling up with thousands of milling students. Some had pitched makeshift tents, a few were gathered in small groups, and others were just standing around looking exhausted.

We arrived at the Capitol on the east Senate side. We walked in but found that the chamber was locked. The president then tried to get into the office he had used as vice president, but this too was locked. In some frustration, he turned around and gestured to us to follow him. He then led us over to the side of the House of Representatives. Our group at this point included the president, Dr. Tkach, Manolo Sanchez, and Robert Taylor, the Secret Service head of the president's detail, who had joined us. I was feeling better now that we were in a safe government building and our protection was increasing.

When we arrived at the House side, we located a man by the name of Frazer who was a custodian. He found a key and led us into the House chamber. What happened next was more surreal than what we had already experienced. The president found the seat he had used as a member of the House. He showed Manolo Sanchez the bullet holes caused during an attack by Puerto Ricans many years before. He then directed Sanchez to go up and sit in the Speaker's chair. "No, no, Mr. President. I shouldn't do that," he protested. "Yes, go on up, Manolo, and give a speech!" With that instruction, Sanchez slowly walked up the steps and, very embarrassed, said a few words about being happy to be an American. The president applauded, as did Dr. Tkach. I was too dumbfounded to react.

We left the House chamber and headed back over to the Senate side. As we were walking through Statuary Hall, the president gestured to me to come over and walk next to him. We all stopped when a tall, elderly, strikingly beautiful black woman who had been mopping the floor came over to him and asked him to sign her Bible. She told him that her name was Carrie Moore. As he signed it, the president told her that he was glad she carried her Bible with her, and he added that "the trouble is that most of us don't read it enough." She answered firmly, "Mr. President, I read it all the time." What happened next opened a window into the president's soul and showed me something that I hadn't seen before. He stood there for a moment, holding her hand. Finally he said, still holding her hand, "You know, my mother was a saint. She died two years ago. She was a saint." There was a lump in his throat when he said, still holding her hand, "You be a saint too."

She answered, looking straight at him, with kind eyes, "I'll try, Mr. President."

The president had just emphasized to the students at the Lincoln Memorial the importance of addressing the spiritual hunger that we all have. And here he was, perhaps reaching out from his own spiritual hunger, holding the hand of Carrie Moore, an obviously deeply religious woman. He shared his feeling that his mother was a saint and encouraged her to be one too. I was moved by this simple, sweet, and gentle encounter in the morning quiet of Statuary Hall and the chance to observe a softer side of Nixon that I had not seen before.

When we got back to the Senate side, we discovered that the chamber was still locked, as was the vice presidential office. We walked out the east Senate entrance and were greeted by Bob Haldeman, Dwight Chapin, and Ron Zeigler, who had just arrived in their car. I felt like the cavalry had finally arrived to rescue the doomed troops. The president got in his limousine, and Haldeman directed me to get in and sit in the jump seat. He went around to the left side and got in sitting next to the president. We pulled out, took a fast right turn onto Constitution Avenue, and headed back to the White House. Or so I thought.

The time was about 6:40 A.M., and the president was now hungry (we had failed to find a place to eat in the Capitol). He said to Taylor, "Bob, let's go over to the Mayflower Hotel. They'll be open for breakfast." "Yes, sir, Mr. President," he answered. In about five minutes, we arrived at the Mayflower. The president, Bob Haldeman, Dr. Tkach, Manolo Sanchez, Dwight Chapin, Ron Zeigler, and I all trooped in as the first patrons of the day. Several astonished waitresses came over to take our orders. I have no recollection of what I ordered, or if I ate it, but the president ordered a poached egg on corned beef hash. As we were eating, he looked down the table at me and asked, "Bud, did you call

Ehrlichman this morning?" "Yes, sir, I did. Right after you called for a car," I answered. "That was too early to call anyone," he responded with an edge in his voice. "Yes, sir, it was early," I agreed.

We left the Mayflower about forty-five minutes later, and several waitresses and hotel employees stood outside waving at us. The president then decided that he was going to walk back to the White House. I moved up alongside of him and told him that there was no way to walk in. In my earlier inspection of the White House perimeter, I had noticed that a Vietcong flag had been hung from an office building on the northwest corner of Lafayette Park. I didn't think it would be a good idea for him to see that flag just then, and I wanted some time to see if we could get it removed peacefully. He continued walking down Connecticut Avenue toward K Street, with his limousine cruising slowly alongside. Traffic had been stopped, so we had the street to ourselves. I looked over to Haldeman, who silently mouthed the words, "Stop him!" I then took the president's left arm and pulled him back. "Sir," I said, realizing at once that I had invaded his personal space, "we can't walk back. We've set it up so that only cars can get into the White House on E Street." He pulled his arm free, glowered at me, and turned around and got into his limousine. Bob Taylor looked across the car at me and gave me a slight nod of approval. I went around and got in the jump seat.

We made good time with full motorcycle support and a chase car back to the White House. As we drove to the White House using the E Street route, the president noticed the barricade of buses for the first time. It had been pitch-dark when he left three hours before. He turned to Haldeman and asked, "Whose idea are all these goddamn buses?" Without missing a beat, Haldeman answered, "They're Bud's idea, sir." "Uh, oh, all right, I see," the president replied.

We swept up the driveway and stopped in front of the map room south entrance to the White House. We got out, and the president walked directly to his office. I turned to Haldeman and said, "Well, I guess he's pretty angry, Bob. I called Ehrlichman too early, physically assaulted him outside the Mayflower, and thought up the buses. Three strikes and you're out, huh?" Haldeman looked at me, smiled, and said, "Don't worry at all. You did everything right. Now, before it all slips away, go over and type as much as you can remember of what just happened." It was 7:30 A.M.

Following Nixon to the Lincoln Memorial and to the Capitol that early morning, at the beginning of a major protest against his decision to invade Cambodia, enabled me to see a deeper side of his character than had been visible to me so far. I saw him in an exposed, emotionally raw state. While he was obviously under enormous stress from the decision he had made that week, there he was, in the middle of a group of young people who had come to demonstrate against him personally, trying to reach out and explain the reasons for his decision. He was trying to empathize with them by explaining that he had felt as they did when he was a poor young student just before World War II. In a way, I felt as though Nixon was a father trying to comfort his children.

His comment to the students that the most important things in life are spiritual resonated powerfully with me, as I too had always felt that spiritual things were the most important. It took a crisis and a most unlikely setting for these deeper ideas to come out of him. Even though I was stressed about my performance that morning, I felt more devoted to him than ever before. I had seen the man behind the mask.

CHAPTER 8

Ensnared in Watergate by Blind Loyalty

During the last week of October 1971, John Dean, the president's counsel, informed me that Jeb Magruder was looking for legal help with some sort of intelligence program at the Committee to Reelect the President (CREEP). I was unhappy with the clandestine activities we had carried out, and I also felt that this was more naturally an opportunity for Liddy, since working in the presidential campaign would use skills that he had already developed as a candidate while running for office in New York's Twenty-eighth Congressional District. I asked him to meet with me and Dean, who would explain to him what Magruder had in mind.

After explaining the scope of the potential political intelligence operation and the substantial money it would need, Dean indicated that Liddy would need to leave the White House to carry it out. I agreed. Liddy told me that he had come to the White House because of Mitchell, that he worked for Ehrlichman and me, and that he wanted assurance that his going to CREEP had everyone's approval. I checked with Ehrlichman, who in turn got Mitchell's concurrence to offer Liddy the position of general counsel to the 1972 campaign. Liddy was now on his way out of the SIU and the White House. After arrangements for his move to CREEP had been made, I called Magruder and told him that Liddy would require close supervision. I did not go into any detail, which I regret, but I did indicate that close monitoring of Liddy's activities would be important.

In early December 1971, a leak appeared in Jack Anderson's column in the *Washington Post* regarding the India-Pakistan conflict. There was information suggesting that the source of the leak was within the National Security Council (NSC) staff.

At the beginning of the investigation, David Young felt that it was necessary to put a warrantless national security wiretap on the home telephone of a yeoman who worked on the NSC staff. We had learned that this staffer had reproduced documents from Kissinger's briefcase and made them available to an admiral assigned to the NSC staff by the chairman of the Joint Chiefs of Staff. This raised the specter that there was a Pentagon spy ring set up to steal secrets from the NSC.

In my view, the warrantless wiretap did not appear to be necessary. I received a call from Ehrlichman while I was attending a meeting at one of the office buildings on Lafayette Square. He asked me whether I agreed with Young's recommendation to institute the wiretap. I said I did not, and he told me that as of that time I was relieved of any further participation in the SIU and that Young would carry on this task by himself.

I learned later that Young completed an extremely thorough and comprehensive investigation, amassing a foot-thick stack of documents, including the results of the wiretaps, interrogations, and cables related to this operation. This massive report on the investigation has never been made available to the public. In their book *Silent Coup*, Len Colodny and Bob Getlin recount the story of this investigation, which they derived from other sources.

The Watergate story has been thoroughly described in many books, with excellent coverage in *All the President's Men* by Bob Woodward and Carl Bernstein. Many principals— Ehrlichman, Magruder, Liddy, even Nixon—wrote biographies with their opinions about Watergate and what happened. From the perspective of those in the White House, it was a difficult, chaotic time.

On June 19, 1972, a story appeared in the *St. Louis Post-Dispatch*. I remember walking through the Chase Park Plaza Hotel in St. Louis, where I was staying for a while attending a seminar. The front-page story caught my eye. It detailed who had been caught in a break-in at the Watergate Hotel in D.C. While I had no knowledge of the planning for or execution of the Watergate break-in, I speculated that by sheer force of his will, Gordon Liddy had persuaded Jeb Magruder, the deputy campaign manager at CREEP, to approve a break-in at the Watergate complex.

At the conclusion of the seminar, I asked my wife Suzanne to join me in St. Louis so that we could drive back to D.C. together. On the way back we stopped over in southern Indiana. Because I had been out of touch for two weeks, I put a call through to the White House for an update on what was happening. My secretary told me that Dean was trying urgently to get in touch with me.

I called Dean, and what he said caused me to recoil. He said we had some major problems brewing based on some "activities" that had happened. He was very cryptic, but I understood exactly what he meant. I went back to the car and told Suzanne about Dean's fears. At that time I hadn't told her the full extent of what I had been involved in, since so much of what we did was kept secret even from our own families.

After returning to D.C., I met with Dean right away. He gave me some background on what had happened in the Watergate event and told me that he had become aware of some of the activities of the SIU in 1971. I told him that it was my belief that everything we did in 1971 was of the highest national security importance and that I still believed that to be true. Dean said that the White House strategy was to suppress any information that would link Watergate with the White House or anything that had occurred the previous year.

I told Dean that I felt bound by the secrecy requirement that had been imposed on the Special Investigations Unit, and that everything I had done had been done under intense pressure to achieve results because of the high national security stakes emphasized by the president. This pressure had come directly from the Oval Office. He nodded as I said this and told me that we were going to have a rough ride.

During the course of the Watergate investigation, U.S. Attorney Earl Silbert decided to question some White House staffers on their knowledge about Watergate. Dean arranged for some staff members to be interviewed rather than required to go before a grand jury. He arranged for me to be interviewed at the Department of Justice by an assistant U.S. attorney. Dean told me that he had secured the agreement of the U.S. attorney that no questions related to national security would be asked, and that if any national security questions were asked, I would have to avoid answering them. He made it clear that disclosure of any of the SIU activities in 1971 would be dangerous and unacceptable. Dean specifically advised me that the Fielding incident was not relevant to Watergate and would not be touched upon in the deposition.

The assistant U.S. attorney who conducted the deposition told me that he was not interested in pursuing national security matters. During the course of the deposition, however, I was asked if I had any knowledge of travel by Hunt and Liddy to California in

1971. I answered the questions by interpreting them as referring to national security, so I said I wasn't aware of any travel to California. As I pointed out in my statement to the court in 1974, "This interpretation was highly strained, reflecting a desperate effort on my part to avoid any possible disclosure of the work of the unit in accordance with the instructions of the President that had been relayed to me by Mr. Ehrlichman." This was confirmed by Dean just before the deposition.

The reason for the question about the California travel? The U.S. attorney was in possession of the photograph that had been left in the camera by Liddy and Hunt. The photograph had been forwarded to the DOJ by the CIA.

After the deposition, I had no further contact with the U.S. attorney or anyone else regarding the work of the SIU. From my perspective at the time, it was a finished operation. I felt that those who had been involved in it—Young, Liddy, Hunt, the Cuban Americans—were all subject to the same secrecy requirements that I was. I also felt, perhaps naively, that this secrecy requirement would carry through any of the investigations into Watergate that involved some of the former SIU members.

The task of implementing the strategy of suppressing knowledge of White House involvement in any of those activities fell to Dean. He received that thankless task even though (as far as I know) he had had no involvement in any of the actual criminal acts of the SIU in 1971 or of the Watergate team from CREEP in 1972.

Following the 1972 election, which Nixon won overwhelmingly against Senator George McGovern, I felt a great desire to leave the White House and serve in one of the departments far removed from law enforcement, narcotics control, or clandestine activity. While I had told my friend Ray Hanzlik, a former schoolmate and colleague on the White House staff, that only a yo-yo would take a position in the Department of Transportation (DOT), I had become increasingly interested in transportation policy. As White House liaison to the District of Columbia, I had worked to resuscitate the appropriations bill for the D.C. Metro, which had been stalemated in Congress.

When I told Ehrlichman about my interest in Transportation, he wasn't initially enthusiastic. He told me that I would have to explain to the president why I wanted to go to DOT, and he arranged for me to take a helicopter ride to Camp David three weeks after the election, when Nixon was in deep retreat preparing for his second term. When I got to Camp David and went to the president's cabin, Manolo Sanchez ushered me into the living room. The president was sitting a few feet away from a crackling fire. He smiled and waved me to the chair opposite him.

"So why do you want to go over to Transportation?"

I told him that I felt Transportation was dealing with some of the more interesting domestic issues that I had been involved in. Although it was a new department, I thought it had a great mission in funding urban mass transit and upgrading the federal aviation system, and I had always had great respect for the Coast Guard. I told the president that I had really enjoyed my work on the White House staff, but that I wanted to participate more directly with Congress and the many interest groups that were engaged in transportation policy.

He looked at me without much enthusiasm, then said, "Well, if that's what you want, it's okay with me." In a later memo, Bob Haldeman wrote that the president felt there were more important things for "Bud to do," but that he (Haldeman) thought going to Transportation was a good idea for now.

When I left Camp David, I was assured that the president would send my nomination forward to the Senate very quickly. I was nominated for the position of undersecretary of Transportation in December 1972.

Lynn Sutcliffe, one of my best friends from law school, was also working in D.C. at that time. He had been editor in chief while I had been notes editor of the *University of Washington Law Review*, and he was now a senior staff member on the Senate Commerce Committee. As soon as Lynn received the nomination, he started preparing the questions that I would be asked in an open hearing before the Senate Commerce Committee.

The Watergate investigation was in full swing, and I was clearly concerned about the kind of questions that I might get. Fortunately, I had had no contact with Liddy since he left the White House in December 1971, so there was no record of discussion with him about Watergate that could have been used to justify questions by the senators on the committee.

The day that I testified before the committee was one of the more intense days of my life. A good friend of mine who had served on the D.C. City Council, Tedson Myers, gave very supportive opening remarks about my nomination. Tedson was one of the finest men I had ever known. He and I had worked on many issues related to the District of Columbia, including law enforcement and his initiative to make the walkways of the District suitable for handicapped people. Some other introductory comments were offered by senators Warren Magnuson and Henry "Scoop" Jackson because I was a resident of Washington State.

Most of the questions from the senators focused on transportation issues that I would face as undersecretary. However, I did get some questions about the organization and activities of the SIU. I answered all of them accurately and truthfully and denied any knowledge of any bugging or electronic surveillance by the SIU. I had been removed from the unit before any of those activities took place. At the end of all the questioning, I received unanimous confirmation for my position as undersecretary of Transportation in January 1973.

On February 4, 1973, Suzanne and I dined as guests of the president at an elegant, formal, seven-course, candlelit dinner in the state dining room of the White House. Each table was attended by two formally dressed waiters and waitresses who served each course and filled our glasses. For most of the people in attendance, it was a festive evening of tinkling crystal, shared memories of the previous five years, and warm toasts—but not for me. Although I was there to celebrate my confirmation as undersecretary of Transportation, as well as the confirmations of my fellow cabinet and subcabinet colleagues, my mood at dinner, far from ebullient, was dark and full of foreboding. The dinner was the culmination of my quest for high position and power that had begun five years before and had now resulted in my appointment as an undersecretary at the age of thirty-three. Unlike most of the celebrants that evening, however, a few others and I were skating on ice slowly melting from the heat of the Watergate investigation.

In May 1973, the ice cracked open and I fell through. Then, after months of guilt and sleepless nights, a Thanksgiving trip to Williamsburg in late November 1973 made me face the errors in my thinking as the head of the SIU.

PART III

Consequences

CHAPTER 9

Pleading Guilty

In *Man's Search for Meaning*, Viktor Frankl asserts that in every situation there is only one right answer. The challenge is figuring out how to work your way through to it. And that one right answer, no matter how difficult a choice, is the answer that will have the greatest integrity.

In the late afternoon of November 23, 1973, I stood on the lawn of the House of Burgesses, the former legislature in Colonial Williamsburg, Virginia. At the invitation of the president of the College of William and Mary and his wife, I had brought my family to Williamsburg as a respite from the Watergate storms that had deluged Washington, D.C.

This was a difficult time. My despair over the course of my legal defense was causing me sharp pangs of conscience. On May 2, 1973, not even four months into the job, I had resigned from my position as undersecretary of Transportation, a casualty of the exploding Watergate investigation.

When I approved the covert operation in Dr. Lewis Fielding's office in 1971, national security was my main concern; I had been able to convince myself that it was the right thing to do under the circumstances. Later, in 1972, I relied on national security to justify lying to an assistant U.S. attorney during the

Watergate investigation about my knowledge of the Plumbers' activities.

As I prepared my defense, again, national security was my justification. But as I worked through the issues, I felt uncomfortable with the soundness of this defense. The more I tried to align my thought with a higher sense of right, the more problematic it became.

Looking around me, I recognized that my family and I were benefiting from rights that emanated from the founding ideals of America. Despite being under indictment in both federal and state courts and publicly identified with serious crimes, I enjoyed the freedom to travel wherever I wanted, to speak with whomever I wished, to pray freely in any church, and to talk to the press. Benefiting from all these rights, I had nonetheless violated another man's civil rights in order to protect the country. This seemed hypocritical regardless of my belief that it had been in the best interests of national defense.

I came to accept that I could no longer defend my conduct. If I defended myself further, if I continued to justify violating rights I continued to enjoy, I would be not only a hypocrite but a traitor to the fundamental American idea of the right of an individual to be free from unwarranted government intrusion in his life. It was then and there, in Colonial Williamsburg, surrounded by family and a sense of the history of America, that I decided to plead guilty.

Three days later my attorney, Steve Shulman, and I walked into the reception room of the office of Leon Jaworski, the special prosecutor for Watergate and related crimes. While I was convinced of the rightness of my decision in Williamsburg, I felt nervous and a little fearful as to how the meeting would go.

Jaworski had been appointed the special prosecutor six weeks before our meeting, after President Nixon had accepted the resignations of Attorney General Elliot Richardson and Deputy Attorney General William Ruckelshaus for their refusal to fire Archibald Cox, the previous special prosecutor. (These dismissals became known as the "Saturday Night Massacre.") Jaworski had a reputation for toughness and fairness, partly from his work on the U.S. prosecution staff at the war crimes trials in Nuremberg, Germany. During my meeting with him that day, and on other occasions several years later, I also learned that he was a compassionate man who deeply loved his country and hated those who abused its trust.

After waiting a few minutes—instead of the standard hour that prosecutors often make suspects wait—Jaworski welcomed me into his stark temporary office. We were joined by William Merrill, the lawyer directly assigned to prosecute the White House Plumbers.

Steve explained to the prosecutors that we had reviewed and analyzed my case from every possible perspective. He told them that we had reached a decision to initiate steps with the special prosecutor that would settle the various charges without requiring a criminal trial. After a few quiet moments, Jaworski asked, "Is this your view, Mr. Krogh?"

"Yes, sir, it is."

"Would you please tell me how you came to this decision?"

I told Jaworski that ever since the president had set up the Special Investigations Unit in 1971 and John Ehrlichman assigned me to it, I had justified what we did on the basis of national security. The president himself had described the work of our unit as being crucial to national security. That was why I'd thought that getting all the information we could about Daniel Ellsberg and his reasons for releasing the Pentagon Papers was serving a national security purpose. And since covert operations had been done in the past for national security, I felt that a covert entry into Dr. Fielding's office to get information about Ellsberg was justifiable. I added that the more I had thought about it, the more clearly I had seen that even though there may well have been some damaging impacts on the national security from Ellsberg's release of the Pentagon Papers, those impacts simply could not justify the invasion of Fielding's rights that this operation involved. I said I didn't feel I could defend my conduct any further because it violated a fundamental principle in our country: the right of an individual to be protected from an unlawful action by his government.

Jaworski and Merrill listened intently to what I said. It was clear that they had discussed the procedure involved in my pleading guilty to the underlying constitutional crimes—deprivation of Dr. Fielding's civil rights to be free from an unlawful search.

"I think we need to get a little more specific, Mr. Krogh. Do I understand that you are prepared to plead guilty to deprivation of Fielding's rights? Is that so?" said Jaworski.

Steve, who seemed to feel that this was moving more quickly than he was comfortable with as my lawyer, jumped into the conversation. He said to Jaworski that I felt I could no longer defend in conscience the Fielding break-in on the basis of national security. He hoped that if we could come to an agreement on my pleading guilty to the deprivation of civil rights charges, the false declaration indictment would be dismissed. He hoped that if I pled guilty to the civil rights charge, which carried a potential ten-year prison sentence, more than any of the lesser charges, that the lesser federal and state charges would be dropped.

For the first time in a long time, the rightness of my decision felt unambiguous. With a guilty plea, however, would come the sentencing process, and in that process I wanted to avoid any possible suggestion that I was seeking leniency through testifying. I believed that the truth was of paramount importance, but that it would be wrong for me to benefit directly from sharing a truth that would damage others. I was concerned about how Jaworski and Merrill would respond to my thoughts on the matter, but unless I had their agreement, I couldn't go forward with my plea.

I made it very clear that my plea of guilty was conditional on the prosecutors' agreement that I would not talk with them or the grand jury until after I'd been sentenced. It was critically important to me that Judge Gerhard Gesell sentence me solely on the basis of what I did, not for what I might say that would implicate others. Even though I understood that others were eager to testify and give up evidence in exchange for a lighter sentence, I couldn't stand the idea. I gave him my word that once sentenced, I would tell them the truth.

Jaworski and Merrill assured me that they would think about my offer to plead guilty before testifying and get back to me quickly. After some hesitation, Jaworski asked me if I had heard of Albert Speer and how he dealt with the prosecution at Nuremberg. He went on to explain that while the gravity of Albert Speer's actions in Hitler's Third Reich made his case vastly different, there was a similar principle at stake: we are all responsible for our own actions, and we can't justify criminal conduct on the basis that we were ordered to do so or felt compelled by circumstances. Jaworski said that those who prosecuted Speer (including Jaworski) had felt that he made an honest effort to take some responsibility for his actions. It sounded to Jaworski as though my offer to plead guilty was an effort to do the same thing. I remembered that Speer was sentenced to twenty years in Spandau prison for his war crimes. I hoped that I would get less than the ten-year possible sentence for the crime I had committed.

One of the most important points I made to Jaworski was that while I felt I was not *exclusively* responsible for what the Plumbers did, I was nevertheless *fully* responsible. Although the idea for the Fielding break-in originated with E. Howard Hunt and G. Gordon

Liddy, I fully endorsed their recommendation. In fact, I had pushed them hard to take aggressive action without fully understanding what that might entail. Because I could have stopped the operation and didn't, I was fully responsible.

We left, and the next morning Steve called and asked me to come see him right away. During our darkest days together during the previous six months, Steve had always maintained a light spirit. At considerable financial sacrifice to himself, he had taken my case at the request of my friend Tedson Meyers. Despite the seriousness of our talks, Steve occasionally lightened things up with one-arm push-up competitions. As I'd crumple to the floor, Steve would continue counting into the twenties, then switch arms.

Steve told me that Jaworski had accepted my offer to plead guilty and that November 30 was the day we would go before Judge Gesell to enter the guilty plea. Steve added that Jaworski was willing to drop the false declaration charge, since the violation of Dr. Fielding's constitutional rights under the Fourth Amendment was much more serious and important than the false declaration charge.

In preparation for the plea in front of Judge Gesell, Steve and I wrote a statement to read in court. A few days later, we walked through a swarm of reporters, photographers, and cameramen and into the E. Barrett Prettyman Federal Courthouse in Washington, D.C. The courtroom was packed with reporters and other regular observers who had followed all of the Watergate press conferences, hearings, and court dramas like groupies trailing a rock band. Standing in front of Judge Gesell, with Steve Shulman at my side, I read the following statement:

> The sole basis for my defense was to have been that I acted in the interest of national security. However, upon serious and

lengthy reflection, I now feel that the sincerity of my motivation cannot justify what was done and that I cannot in conscience assert national security as a defense. I am therefore pleading guilty because I have no defense to this charge. I will make a detailed statement as to my reasons which I will submit to the Court and make public prior to sentencing. . . .

My decision is based upon what I think and feel is right and what I consider to be the best interests of the nation. The values expressed by your Honor in the hearing on defense motions on November 13 particularly brought home to me the transcendent importance of the rule of law over the motivations of man.

I have expressed to the Special Prosecutor's office my desire that I not be required to testify in this area until after sentencing. My plea today is based on conscience, and I want to avoid any possible suggestion that I am seeking leniency through testifying. The Special Prosecutor's office has expressed no objection to this position.

My coming to this position today stems from my asking myself what ideas I wanted to stand for, what I wanted to represent to myself and to my family and to be identified with for the rest of my experience. I simply feel that what was done in the Ellsberg operation was in violation of what I perceive to be the fundamental idea in the character of this country—the paramount importance of the rights of the individual. I don't want to be associated with that violation any longer by attempting to defend it.

I had finally reached an understanding of the hole in my decision-making process—that what I had done wasn't right and that it had had a hugely negative impact on society. Despite the fear of what prison and life as a convicted felon might hold, my final decision to plead guilty was an important step in restoring some of my integrity.

A few weeks later I sat down with former White House special counsel Charles Colson, his Christian colleagues, and Senator Harold Hughes at Fellowship House in Washington, D.C. During our prayer meeting I had explained to them why I felt it essential that I plead guilty and serve whatever sentence might be imposed. I was willing to accept any punishment that a court might impose. Moreover, as I had indicated to my friend David Eisenhower, I had pleaded guilty on the basis of conscience and did not want to be pardoned. Serving a prison sentence was an opportunity for me to pay part of the price that had to be paid for my misconduct.

Perhaps the most important part of my thought process had been to step outside of the circumstances in which I made my original decision. Specifically, I could see that my absolute loyalty to President Nixon personally and to his view of the national security threat had skewed my perspective. This kind of absolute loyalty lacked integrity, I came to understand, because it was unbalanced and too exclusive. Loyalty to the president was obviously important up to a point. However, loyalty to the Constitution, to the rule of law, and to moral and ethical requirements should have been key factors in my decisions as well.

In addition, groupthink had infected the decision making of the Plumbers' unit. Each of us brought to the work of the unit a high degree of zeal. We accepted the description of the threat without question, and we did not question each other on the rightness of the break-in or its necessity.

National security as I perceived it in 1971 was a monolithic concept. I accepted that if the president invoked that term, then the threat to the nation's security was substantial and immediate. Upon pleading guilty, I realized that the term cannot be used as a blanket justification for any type of conduct to defend the nation's security.

Six weeks later, before sentencing, I wrote to Judge Gesell in my "Statement of Defendant on the Offense and His Role" that "national security is obviously a fundamental goal and a proper concern of any country. It is also a concept that is subject to a wide range of definitions, a factor that makes all the more essential a painstaking approach to the definition of national security in any given instance." In responding to the national security threat as more clearly defined, government investigators must make painstaking efforts to ensure that they are complying with the law.

Perhaps the simplest way to reach the right decision at the time would have been to ask people I knew who had real integrity whether this was the right decision. In the environment of secrecy within the White House, however, such advice would have been extremely difficult to seek.

At my sentencing hearing on January 24, 1974, I told Judge Gesell how deeply sorrowful I was over the suffering that many people had endured because of my offense. I noted that both Lewis Fielding and Daniel Ellsberg had been deprived of rights to which they were entitled. I explained that the American people had been confused and disturbed by what took place in the Fielding break-in and by the many questions it raised about what the country represented and what it meant. I said that no assertion of national security, no matter how deeply held, could change the fact that I had made a fundamental mistake.

Judge Gesell listened carefully and then responded:

> Contrary to the public understanding, you were not involved in any other aspect of the various events being investigated by the Special Watergate Prosecutor. You received no money for your

part in this affair. In acknowledging your guilt, you have made no effort, as you very well might have, to place the primary blame on others who initiated and who approved the undertaking. A wholly improper, illegal task was assigned to you by higher authority and you carried it out because of a combination of loyalty and I believe a degree of vanity, thereby compromising your obligations as a lawyer and as a public servant.

He then placed his decision in a broader legal context, quoting Justice Brandeis: "If the Government becomes a lawbreaker, it breeds contempt for the law. It invites every man to become a law unto himself. It invites anarchy."

The judge told me that because I was a lawyer and had held high responsibility when the offense occurred, any punishment short of jail would be inadequate. He then sentenced me to a term of two to six years of which I was to serve six months and remain on unsupervised probation for another two years.

■

Precisely eight months later, on August 24, 1974, two weeks after his resignation, Richard Nixon and I met in San Clemente. During a two-hour discussion, he asked me whether he had approved the break-in of Fielding's office. Perhaps he was unclear which break-ins he had knowledge of and had authorized. When I told him, no, he had not, to my knowledge, approved the covert operation into Fielding's office, he told me that had I asked him for his approval, I would have had it. But for me, by then, that was hardly the point.

CHAPTER 10

From Courthouse
to Jailhouse

"**A**re the cuffs too tight?" The United States marshal, a black man with kind eyes, finished handcuffing me to a waist chain linked to shackles around each of my ankles. He had just led me from a solitary holding cell in the basement of the E. Barrett Prettyman Federal Courthouse in Washington, D.C., to a covered concourse where prisoners were driven in and out. At my sentencing hearing ten days before, U.S. District Judge Gerhard Gesell had directed me to turn myself in to the U.S. marshals.

"No, not too tight," I answered. He gently took my arm and led me clanking to the standard-issue government sedan. He put his hand on my head as I ducked down and eased me into the backseat. The marshal and his partner, the driver, got in the front seat. The driver started the car immediately and pulled quickly out of the concourse, taking a left turn past a few lingering photographers and reporters milling around the entrance. He turned right onto Pennsylvania Avenue for a few blocks, skirted the Ellipse south of the White House and my former office, and headed northwest out the George Washington Parkway toward the Montgomery County jail in Rockville, Maryland.

As I was driven to Rockville, I reflected on the awful irony of going to jail for committing a serious federal crime when one of my principal responsibilities had been to reduce crime in the District of Columbia. Judge Gesell had sentenced me to two to six years in prison, suspending all of it except for six months, for violating the civil rights of Dr. Lewis Fielding, Dr. Daniel Ellsberg's psychiatrist.

For the brief four months I served as undersecretary of the Department of Transportation in 1973, I was provided "portal-to-portal" service. I was picked up at my home by a DOT driver, usually around 7:00 A.M., taken to the department headquarters building, and then driven home at the end of the day. Being driven from the Prettyman courthouse to the Rockville jail gave "portal-to-portal" a whole new meaning.

About forty minutes after leaving the courthouse, we arrived at the Rockville jail. A maximum-security facility, the jail is located in a one-story concrete building just below Seven Locks Road in a shallow ravine. The marshal who had cuffed me opened the back door and helped me get out and stand up. He escorted me into the intake center at the back of the jail. Once inside, and after handing over some documentation to the officer and getting a receipt, he unfastened and removed my handcuffs. Because the U.S. Bureau of Prisons contracts with local county jails to house federal prisoners temporarily while awaiting transfers to a federal facility, I was now in the custody of the Montgomery County, Maryland, jail system. I didn't know how long I was going to be there, or if or where I would be sent to serve out the six months of imprisonment Judge Gesell had imposed.

"Good luck," the marshal said as he turned and left.

"Thanks," I replied. I felt he meant it.

The intake officer and two other jail officials told me to go into a small room and take off my clothes. After one of them completed a body search, the other gave me a khaki shirt and pants to put on and directed me to keep my underwear and shoes and socks. I was taken from the intake room through a steel door and down a short hall to a temporary holding cell.

The holding cell was a rectangle about fifteen feet by twenty feet, with floor-to-ceiling bars on two sides and a heavy barred door set in one side. The officer unlocked the door and gestured me into the cell. A stand-up urinal was wedged in the corner, framed by mattresses on the floor shoved up against the walls. A black man with a badly bruised face sat on the mattress to the right of the urinal and looked up at me as I stepped in. I heard the door clang shut behind me and the key turn in the lock. I had to choose where to sit.

Despite some fear, an inner impulsion prompted me to walk over and sit down on the mattress next to the first cell occupant. Neither of us spoke for about a minute. We just sat there quietly. Finally, he raised his head, turned, looked at me out of the corner of his swollen eye, and said:

"Krogh, I liked the way you did that. You just came over and sat down next to me. I know all about you. You're a stand-up guy. Now I'm going to teach you how to live in jail."

I looked at him as he said this. I was stunned and frightened that the first prisoner I met in jail knew my name and all about my case. The odds were overwhelmingly stacked against such a coincidence, and I worried about what I might encounter later. He smiled at my shocked look and said that he had followed my case on TV. He then said he was going to give me some rules for surviving in jail.

The rules were basic and simple. Keep to yourself until you know the situation. Don't get in anyone's space or hide in a corner either. Don't look anyone directly in the eye right away until you know him, because it might be taken as a threat. Don't talk to the jailers or someone will think you're working for them and that's bad. He said—and I remember his words as if they were spoken yesterday—"You come in here as a white man, a lawyer, a Nixon dude. Don't you never hold yourself out better than anyone else in here. Don't do it because someone will hurt you if you do. And don't do it because it just ain't true."

These and other rules, a crash course in Jail Survival 101, flowed out of him over the next half-hour. I asked about the daily routine, food, visitors, reading materials. He gave me good, helpful answers. A jailer came to the cell all too soon and summoned me to get up and follow him. I shook my friend's hand and thanked him, for he had extended himself in friendship to me, and I followed the jailer out of the cell. I never saw this friend again.

The jailer led me out of the holding cell and down a corridor to a room stacked with mattresses, bedding, and towels. He told me to pick up a vinyl-covered mattress, sheets, and a towel. Carrying these items, I followed him to a larger detention unit in the back corner of the jail. He inserted his key in the steel door, then directed me into a large, cagelike cell that was to be my home for the next ten days.

This cell, with light green walls and a dark green floor, had three steel picnic-style tables and benches bolted to the floor, an open shower, two open commodes, and a sink in the first section. A television set was bolted onto a steel platform about seven feet up near the steel door. Two rows of steel double bunks stretched into the back section of the cell. I walked to the end of the row of bunks on the right and tossed my mattress onto the top bunk springs.

About ten men were in the cell, some at the tables watching television, a few in their bunks. No one acknowledged me as I walked in, and nothing was said. After putting my sheets on the bed, I walked back to the nearest table and found some open space on one of the steel benches. Through the rest of the afternoon, we watched television shows.

The evening news came on around five o'clock, and one of the lead stories showed me, accompanied by my wife Suzanne and my lawyer, Steve Shulman, turning myself in at the courthouse that morning. One fellow inmate looked intently at the screen, over at me, back to the screen, then back at me again.

"Man!!" he said loudly. "I ain't seen no one *walk* into jail before!!" This triggered interest from the other prisoners, who now looked over at me.

"Why didn't you just take off?" he asked.

"Nowhere to go," I answered. I realized that some of these inmates had been arrested at their crime scenes. Taking off for them was a logical thing to do.

"I would have been easily recognized wherever I went. Nowhere to run," I explained further. A couple of them nodded their heads. When I explained the circumstances of my case, one of them said that I didn't belong there.

"Hey, man, you did what you thought was right. You shouldn't be here."

This was dangerous ground, so I countered quickly that I had pleaded guilty to a very serious federal crime. I explained that I had deprived a doctor of his right to be free from an unwarranted search, a big-time constitutional crime, and that was serious stuff. I had to establish my mala fides as a criminal in order to have bona fides as a prisoner. And I applied one of the rules for survival that had just been given me a few hours before: "Don't you never hold yourself out better than anyone else."

Shortly after this conversation, a cart containing our dinners was wheeled outside of the cage and steel trays were handed through a space in the bars. Each tray contained two cold hot dogs, some corn, bread, and a bottled beverage. I was more at ease that evening eating dinner off of a steel plate in a jail cell than I had been exactly one year before at my confirmation dinner in the White House. During that first evening in the Rockville jail, I recalled the imprisoning fear, pressure, and darkness that had shrouded my mood during that White House dinner one year before. There, in the Rockville maximum-security jail, eating cold hot dogs with my fellow prisoners, I finally felt free, in harmony with myself, and at peace.

After ten days in the Rockville jail, I was transferred to Allenwood Federal Prison in White Deer, Pennsylvania, about two hundred miles north of Washington, D.C., in the foothills of the northern Allegheny Mountains. When I arrived there in mid-February 1974, handcuffed and foot-shackled, it was cold and bleak.

New prisoners at Allenwood were given the choice of working in a furniture factory, on the four-thousand-acre prison farm, in food preparation, or on the janitorial staff. At the recommendation of a fellow inmate at Rockville, I asked to be assigned to the Allenwood farm. He had told me that this would enable me to work outdoors. The kinds of farm jobs we did during a typical day included feeding some of the more than one thousand head of cattle, cleaning cattle pens, chopping underbrush, and clearing rocks. Later in the spring, after I had mastered the technique of operating the Massey Ferguson 1105 tractor, I plowed, disked, harrowed, and fertilized several of the fields where corn was to be planted.

On a typical day, I got up at the 6:00 A.M. count and then took my Bible and other spiritual literature to the small smoking room in the common area between the two dormitory wings where over 160 prisoners lived. There I studied and pondered the lives of those biblical figures who had "done time." I remember how moved I was by the story of Joseph in the Book of Genesis. Rather than feel victimized by the terrible circumstances of his life—sold into slavery and imprisoned in Egypt—Joseph always tried to do his best and worked hard wherever he found himself. He didn't whine or complain. He took responsibility for his life. This story inspired me every day to give my best effort, whether working on the farm, helping other prisoners with their legal and family issues, or trying to stay fit by running around the dormitory compound.

Viktor Frankl was another source of inspiration that helped me in prison, especially the ideas in his book *Man's Search for Meaning*. Frankl was an inmate at Auschwitz concentration camp during World War II, and he recounts in this masterpiece of storytelling how he survived that experience. His central idea is that those who have a sense of meaning in their lives can survive practically any hardship. Frankl quotes Nietzsche's line: "He who has a *why* to live can bear almost any *how*." I understood very clearly that the *why* of my experience in the Rockville and Allenwood prisons was to accept full responsibility for the crime to which I had pleaded guilty and thus to complete the legal chain of consequences that taking responsibility required.

One experience Frankl described affected me powerfully. In his barracks at Auschwitz, many inmates had simply given up and decided to die. He explained that the death rate between Christmas 1944 and New Year's 1945 had increased greatly. Many of these prisoners had harbored false hopes that they would be home by Christmas, and when that did not happen, they gave up hope, lost courage, and died. He was asked to speak to his fellow inmates one evening to encourage them not to give up. Specifically, he addressed the argument from those who had given up that "I have nothing to expect from life anymore." What he told them helped me then and has helped me ever since.

What was really needed was a fundamental change in our attitude toward life. We had to learn ourselves and, furthermore, we had to teach the despairing men, that *it did not really matter what we expected from life, but rather what life expected from us.* We needed to stop asking about the meaning of life, and instead to think of ourselves as those who were being questioned by life, daily and hourly. Our answer must consist, not in talk and meditation, but in right action and in right conduct. Life ultimately means taking the responsibility to find the right answer to its problems and to fulfill the tasks which it constantly sets for each individual.

Frankl's answer to the question of what life expects from us—taking responsibility to find the right answer to its problems and then engaging in right conduct—aligns perfectly with one of the key questions that integrity requires: Is it right? While I find that meditation and contemplation are extremely valuable in accessing spiritual truths and giving a clearer understanding of what is right, more than just talk or meditating on the meaning of life is required. It requires action to fulfill the tasks that life sets before us, whatever and wherever they may be.

Following this quiet time on a typical morning, I would join the farm crew for early breakfast, after which we'd pile on the truck that transferred us to the farm barns where our workday began. In the evenings I would read, answer letters, or counsel some of my fellow prisoners.

One evening, after three grueling shifts pulling up and stacking fence posts on the farm, I was sitting on my bunk, head down and exhausted. A good friend who was in the same barracks handed me a copy of the latest *Christian Science Monitor*, telling me that it might cheer me up. I opened it to a page that displayed an oil painting by Rembrandt entitled *Paul in Prison*.

I stared in amazement at the picture. In the painting, Paul is depicted sitting on his bunk in his prison cell in the exact same position I was in sitting on my bunk at Allenwood. An essay entitled "A Free Man," by Neil Millar, adjoined the picture. Millar quoted from a poem, "To Althea: From Prison," by Richard Lovelace, who wrote:

> *Stone walls do not a prison make*
> *Nor iron bars a cage;*
> *Minds innocent and quiet take*
> *That for an hermitage;—*

After the quote, Millar wrote that Paul was "not studying his prison cell. Except as a refuge, it is unimportant. Why should he consider the brief stone walls when his whole universe thrills with the Eternal. He lives in the blaze of conscious immortality, in which a wall is a symbol only, imprisonment a mere punctuation mark in a universal poem of life."

This picture and essay seemed to be directed precisely to my need for encouragement at that moment. I realized that my short prison sentence was a "mere punctuation mark" in the "universal poem" of my life. I was deeply grateful for Lovelace's calming verse and Millar's soaring words, which lifted me out of the gloom I had been feeling.

The best part of each week for me was on Sunday when Suzanne and our two boys, eight-year-old Peter and four-year-old Matthew, would drive the two hundred miles from our home in D.C. to spend three hours with me in the prison visiting room. I missed them terribly. They were always upbeat and lifted my spirits. Pete in particular was impressed that I had learned how to drive a tractor.

While my time in the White House had prepared me for many circumstances in life, it didn't prepare me for what I would see while waiting in line to have my teeth checked and cleaned by the prison dentist. A long queue of prisoners slowly made their way to the dentist's chair. As we approached, I was horrified to realize that the dentist's assistant was a Frenchman I had worked to put behind bars.

As the coordinator of drug programs under Nixon, I had been directed to work on many of the drug-related law enforcement issues of the day. A small part of my work focused on two specific things: the drug conditions prevalent among the troops in Vietnam and French heroin smuggling. This latter work was fictionalized in the Gene Hackman movie *The French Connection*, which told about the American government's work to stop the flow of heroin through Marseilles and on to America. When I saw who the dental assistant was, I realized that my own French connection was about to come full circle.

The assistant, Roger Delouette, waited for me armed with a full complement of sharp metal dental devices. Delouette had been an operative for Jacques Foccart's African diamond trafficking network and an employee of Roger Barberot, the noted French secret agent, ambassador, and heroin trafficker. Delouette was arrested in New Jersey with more than forty kilos of heroin in his car. His confession had led to the breakup of Auguste Ricord's smuggling ring, but also landed him in Allenwood Federal Prison. Under my watch, we had aggressively prosecuted all the drug smugglers we could find, and Delouette had been put away for a long time because of my work.

So when I finally came to the dentist's chair, I knew I could be in big trouble from the armed man now behind bars with me. But rather than attacking me, Delouette laughed and said, "Don't be afraid, Mr. Krogh. We were both professionals, and we both scrrreewwwed up!" Delouette was right. He too was a patriot who had ended up in jail in part because of the sinuous reach of French national security arguments that were obliquely behind his fate.

To be confronted by the inescapable reality of the error of my ways was the first crucial step: it allowed me to accept for sure that I had been in the wrong. What that realization prompted was a further series of questions, all starting from one basic question: *why* had I done wrong?

In the thirty years since the Watergate scandal, I have pondered the reasons for those terrible decisions that took me to Rockville and Allenwood and mulled over the lessons I learned from my time in Washington, D.C. The central question I have tried to answer for myself, and for this book, is why good people make bad decisions. Why do good people, whether in government, business, the professions, the media, or academia, choose courses of action that inflict harm on those we would help, destroy our own careers, or undermine the institutions we serve?

CHAPTER 11

The Road Home

Just after midnight on June 22, 1974, I was released from federal custody. I had served the last two weeks of my prison sentence at Fort Holabird, Maryland, in a fenced, two-story barracks tucked inside the military base. Most of the other prisoners in this facility were in the Justice Department's witness protection program. I was moved from Allenwood Prison in central Pennsylvania to Fort Holabird because the Watergate special prosecutor's office wanted me closer to Washington, D.C., so that they could get access to me quickly. They needed my testimony as part of their criminal cases for conspiracy against John Ehrlichman, G. Gordon Liddy, and E. Howard Hunt for their Plumbers' offenses. In my plea of guilty on November 30, 1973, I had insisted that the court sentence me for my own crime before calling me to testify against any others on the White House staff. Special prosecutor Leon Jaworski agreed to this condition if I would promise to testify truthfully when called as a prosecution witness. This I agreed to do.

After driving out of the gate at Fort Holabird, Suzanne and I decided it would be prudent to spend the night outside of Washington, D.C. In those days the press kept a watchful eye on the trial, imprisonment, and release dates of Nixon White House staff members, and we were not ready to meet the press in the middle of the night. Late the next morning, we drove into our driveway at 6949 Greenvale Street N.W. in Washington, D.C., and were greeted by over a dozen reporters and cameramen. We spoke briefly to them, telling them how good it was to be home. When I walked into our house, I was greeted by a large sign that festooned the entrance and read: WELCOME BACK TO THE HOME OF THE BRAVE AND THE LAND OF THE FREE. Suzanne knew the exact right words for a great homecoming. Both my sons, Pete and Matt, were there, jumping and running around, and we had a joyous reunion.

The next three weeks were spent getting familiar with freedom. Many friends from all over the country called to tell us they loved us and were still pulling for us. Most of them knew that the ordeal of the inevitable attorney discipline proceedings lay ahead of us in Washington State. Bill Dwyer, the attorney in Seattle who had agreed to represent me in the Washington State bar proceedings, informed us that a hearing was being planned for August 20, two short months away. He asked that we come to Seattle several days in advance to prepare.

Bill Dwyer's acceptance of my case for the Washington State bar proceedings was pivotal to any hope I had for practicing law again. On January 24, Judge Gerhard Gesell had acknowledged in his statement when sentencing me to prison that "you are standing at the Bar and hence your ability later to earn a living has already been undoubtedly adversely affected."

Six weeks before Judge Gesell sentenced me, I had met Bill Dwyer for the first time. A close lawyer friend of mine, Keith Dysart, had called me right after I pleaded guilty to tell me that he had spoken with Dwyer and that he had agreed to meet with me. Keith told me that Bill was viewed by many lawyers as one of the best litigating attorneys ever to practice law in Washington

State. He added that he didn't know whether Bill, a liberal Democrat, would accept my case. I trusted Keith's judgment completely. He and I had practiced law briefly together in John Ehrlichman's law firm before I left for the White House staff. During my third year of law school, I was always on call to do research for Keith and other members of the Ehrlichman firm. Keith's calls for help usually came after midnight, as he was by nature a nocturnal creature. He arranged for me to have my own key to the King County Law Library in Seattle so that I could get in after it was closed, do the research, and write the law memos that I would then run over to his office before 5:00 A.M. Keith and I remained close friends over the next few years, so I was confident that if he felt that Bill Dwyer was the best lawyer for me, then Dwyer it would be.

I called Dwyer's office and found out that he would be in Kalamazoo, Michigan, in mid-December 1973 taking depositions on a large antitrust case involving mint growers in Washington State. His secretary arranged for us to meet for two hours in downtown Kalamazoo at a café he frequented regularly.

A few days later I flew up to Kalamazoo in a small commuter plane that was buffeted around in blizzard conditions. When I walked into the café, a very fit, handsome, midsized man wearing a Pendleton shirt, jeans, and a sheepskin coat got up from a booth and came over to shake hands. He introduced himself as Bill Dwyer and invited me to follow him back to his booth. My first impression of Bill Dwyer was of a man deeply at peace with himself. His smile was genuine, his handshake firm, and his voice calm, compassionate, and reassuring.

When we were seated and had ordered lunch, he sat back, smiled, and said, "Okay, Bud, I've been reading about you in the papers. Keith asked me to meet with you, and I'm happy to do so. But I'd like to hear your story as you see it."

Already feeling a great sense of trust and kindness from him, I spoke for about forty-five minutes. I began with law school, detailing all aspects of my work on land reform with Roy Prosterman and then describing my specific assignments on the White House staff, including narcotics control, D.C. affairs, antiwar demonstrations, and transportation policy. I then gave him an account of the Plumbers' operation, concluding with a full explanation of the reasons I had felt compelled to plead guilty to depriving Lewis Fielding of his civil rights. For the next hour he asked questions that I answered as fully as I could. His questions were direct and designed to get me to open up my deepest feelings. It was a most gentle form of cross-examination.

After his last question, he sat back again and thought for a while. I didn't know what to expect. He finally leaned forward and said, "Bud, I'll take your case. But there are some things that are very important right now." First, he warned me that a prison sentence was likely, and he wanted me to serve whatever sentence was imposed as honorably as possible. Second, he did not feel that it was appropriate for me to "capitalize" on the serious constitutional crime that I had committed, so he urged me not to write a book right away that would make money. Third, he said it would be important for me to make amends for my actions, and we would work together to find out how best to do that. Finally, he said that the bar proceedings could take a long time, maybe even years, but "we will eventually prevail." He then reached over, shook my hand, and smiled. I remember being very emotional and thanking him profusely. I felt that a tremendous weight had been lifted off my back and that there was now some prospect that sometime in the future I would be able to practice law again. We walked out of the café together. He told me to keep in touch as best I could over the next few months.

After my return home from prison, press interest shifted quickly to the upcoming trials of my former White House colleagues. The actual experience of testifying against Gordon Liddy and Howard Hunt, two men who had worked for me, and especially John Ehrlichman, my mentor and friend, was absolutely excruciating. David Young, my codirector of the White House Plumbers, had early on been given full immunity by Earl Silbert, the U.S. attorney who had initial responsibility for the Watergate cases. Young's immunity was offered in exchange for the Plumbers' documents and incriminating testimony he would provide later at the trial of Ehrlichman and other defendants. The prosecutors told me that my testimony was of great value because I had already served a prison sentence. While I had not received immunity, I was still obligated to testify truthfully as part of the plea agreement I had reached with Jaworski the previous year.

When I was on the stand as a prosecution witness, the prosecutors led me through a series of questions about the authority that David Young and I had received from John Ehrlichman to carry out a covert operation. I was asked to confirm my initials on the memo from Young and me to Ehrlichman that recommended the operation. In answer to a question on cross–examination, I affirmed that at the time when the Plumbers were operating in 1971, I felt that we were carrying out a mission dictated by a national security requirement. To a question posed by the prosecutor, I said that I had since changed my view and no longer felt that national security could justify what was done. My time on the stand was short—no longer than two hours—and it was a relief to have it over with. One of the most difficult things I have ever had to do in my life was to testify against my friends in a criminal trial. I had little doubt that they would probably be convicted and serve prison sentences, and so it proved. Like me, they were convicted, and they did serve time.

After concluding my testimony, Suzanne and I decided we should take a trip around the country and arrive in Seattle in time to prepare for the first hearing before the bar association panel. But first, we wanted to do something fun with our children. Like many who have gone through challenging times, we decided we should go to Disney World. On the way, we would pick up a cartoon.

During my term at Allenwood, a color cartoon by Ralph Dunagin was pinned up on the prison bulletin board. It depicted an obviously new prisoner sitting on a cot with an older con looking down at him and saying, "Eagle Crow, huh? Say, you're not the famous birdman of Alcatraz, are you?" This led to my being nicknamed "Birdman" by some fellow prisoners. I wrote Dunagin and asked if he would consider giving me the original. He wrote back and said that if I came to his newspaper in Orlando, Florida, after my release from prison, he would be delighted to give it to me.

For a few days we kicked back, rode all the rides we could at Disney World and Epcot, marveled at the acrobatic tricks of whales and dolphins at Marine World, and got caught up with my Orlando friends. Principia College alumni are fiercely loyal to their own, and they live all over the United States and in many other countries. During the previous year, since my case had become public, generous financial support from hundreds of my fellow alums had come to us. The Bud Krogh Legal Defense Fund had been established on my behalf by Jim Morand, a close friend, and Dick Nordahl, a fellow Principia graduate. To pay my legal fees, which ran into the tens of thousands of dollars even without a trial, Suzanne and I exhausted all of our personal financial resources, including my small retirement account from the federal government. The legal defense fund paid for most of the remaining legal bills. I am eternally grateful to those who helped me so much in a time of extraordinary need.

After leaving Orlando, we drove across the country by the southern route, through Alabama, Mississippi, Louisiana, and Texas. We camped several nights in New Mexico and Arizona and arrived in Seattle in late July. Driving across large swaths of America released me from my previous preoccupation with the Watergate scandal and the imprisoning political perspective of Washington, D.C. With my family, I was able to relax and deeply enjoy the greatness, simplicity, and authenticity of the part of America that on the East Coast is often referred to as "fly-over country."

As a boy and later as a law student, I had always enjoyed mountaineering. One dream I had was to climb Mount Rainier, a 14,410-foot volcano an hour away from Seattle. Suzanne and I persuaded my brother-in-law, Don Davis, and two of my nieces, Joelyn and Tishy Davis, to join us in training for a Rainier climb soon after we arrived in Seattle. I felt that it would be a great way to celebrate my new freedom. I also then planned to work closely with Bill Dwyer to prepare for the first hearing before the three-lawyer panel of the Washington State Bar Association that would determine whether I could continue to practice as a lawyer.

During the summer after I was released from prison, I had tried to maintain a high level of physical conditioning by regular jogging. Training for Mount Rainier was very different, however, because a Rainier climb involves carrying heavy packs over snow. Many people who manage to climb Mount Rainier take a mountaineering course from Rainier Mountaineering Inc. (RMI), the climbing outfit that had a guiding concession from Mount Rainier National Park. RMI guides give neophyte climbers lessons in how to rope up, belay, cross a crevassed glacier, and use an ice ax for roped climbing and for self-arrest, and how to save energy by using the "rest" step. I took the course in early August along with Suzanne, my brother-in-law, and my two nieces.

On August 8, a few days after taking the course, we left Paradise Lodge with our RMI team and headed up a four-mile stretch primarily over a snowfield to Camp Muir at 10,000 feet. Arriving at Camp Muir around 4:00 P.M., we moved our packs and sleeping bags into a stone hut with three levels of thick plywood sheets for our beds. After a light dinner, we crawled into our sleeping bags and tried to sleep. But between the excitement over the upcoming climb and the altitude, most of us slept fitfully. At midnight our guides woke us up and after a quick breakfast we headed out across the Cowlitz Glacier around 1:00 A.M. for our summit attempt. As we set out, on August 9, 1974, at 1:00 A.M. Pacific Daylight Time—4:00 A.M. Eastern Daylight Time— Richard Nixon was still president of the United States.

During the next twelve hours, our team rest-stepped slowly up the standard route on Rainier, crossed the Cowlitz and Ingraham Glaciers, and then headed up Disappointment Cleaver. (If ever there was a name of a climbing route designed to discourage and sap the energy of aspiring summit climbers, "Disappointment Cleaver" was it.) At the top of the cleaver, at 12,500 feet, Suzanne decided she would wait for us to come back down. She had been told by one of the guides—erroneously, as we soon discovered—that the pitches that remained above were more difficult than those we had already covered. She would have reached the summit with us if she had been told that the remaining part of the climb was in fact easier. Our remaining group zigzagged back and forth, avoiding deep crevasses, and around 7:00 A.M. we eased onto the eastern summit rim, where we celebrated by drinking pints of water, eating dried fruit, salami, and cheese, and signing the register.

Our descent was slow, as it usually is for first-time summit climbers on Mount Rainier. Most climbers know that coming down is often more difficult than going up. On the last section of the Muir snowfield, a couple of miles above the end of the climb at Paradise Lodge, we saw and then heard another party of about a dozen climbers heading up. As we got closer, we heard them yelling, "We have a new president! We have a new president! Nixon's gone! Ford's in! Nixon's gone! Ford's in!"

"What did you say?" I yelled over to them.

"Nixon just resigned. He's goooooone!!!!" one of them yelled back gleefully.

I stopped in my tracks, took off my pack, and bent over. I was physically tired, but I now felt a huge emotional weight of sadness and regret. My family gathered around, and we just stood quietly together for a few minutes. Right then, standing on a snowfield on Mount Rainier, I decided that it was now time to complete some of the unfinished aspects of my earlier decision to take responsibility for my actions as head of the Plumbers.

CHAPTER 12

Making Amends

With a guilty plea before Judge Gesell and a prison term served as honorably as I could, I had finished paying the minimum debt to society that had been required of me. For the sake of my own integrity and peace of mind, however, I felt the need to make amends to the men whom my actions had damaged the most. This would require that I go to California to apologize to Dr. Lewis Fielding and then to San Clemente to see Richard Nixon.

The impact of my actions on Dr. Fielding had weighed heavily on me since the break-in and also during my time in prison, when the importance of privacy and individual rights in our society became abundantly clear to me. I had violated both Fielding's privacy and his rights, and I now had much more experience of what that could mean on a personal level. Prison, no matter how honorably one serves, is designed to deprive inmates of precisely both these things. The integrity of our society rests in part on the need to trust citizens to act with respect for each other's rights; in prison, that trust is revoked, and I felt the loss keenly, as I was sure Fielding had.

With Richard Nixon, I needed to explain exactly what had happened with the SIU and my part in it. Many have reviled

Nixon, then and now, as at best a ruthless politician, and at worst an evil man who directed the scandals perpetrated during his presidency. For me, however, he had been an important authority figure who often made clear, sometimes brilliant, policy decisions. In the areas that I directly worked on for Nixon—drug control policy, transportation, the District of Columbia—he had enabled me to make decisions and changes that I felt were both important and beneficial. I owed him both thanks and an apology for the impact of my actions on his presidency.

Before I could see Nixon and Fielding, however, I had a deadline to meet. I had to work closely with Bill Dwyer to prepare for and participate in the first hearing that would determine whether I would be able to practice law in Washington State again.

When I arrived in Seattle, Bill Dwyer greeted me warmly in his office. It was the first time I had seen him since our Kalamazoo meeting. He and two associates in his highly respected firm—Culp, Dwyer, Guterson & Grader—had already completed a great deal of research on the issues we would need to address in the upcoming hearing. We spent the next week and a half preparing my testimony for direct examination and contacting and preparing potential witnesses whom we asked to testify on my behalf.

The first issue we had to decide was whether to request that the three-lawyer panel hearing be closed or open to the public. Normally, attorney discipline cases are considered and decided in closed, confidential hearings. I had come to the view by then that excessive secrecy had contributed to some of the misdeeds of the Nixon White House. Public confidence in the process and recommendation of the panel was important, and this would be harder to achieve in a secret hearing. So Bill and I concluded that since the case was already very much in the public arena, and we wanted a full public record, the wisest course was for the hearing to be open to everyone. We recommended this to the bar association. Fortunately, the bar association's superb counsel, Michael Jacobsen, agreed, and he was able to secure agreement from the Board of Governors as well.

The hearing was held in a large room in the King County Courthouse, a large, forbidding building in downtown Seattle. Over a day and a half, twelve witnesses appeared on my behalf. These witnesses included several lawyers who had attended law school with me and a few with whom I had worked in the government. They were uniformly kind in their remarks and offered strong support to our position that I was intellectually and ethically fit to practice law. After the hearing, the three-lawyer panel recommended that I be suspended from the practice of law for nine months.

Bill and I were jubilant with this outcome. While we had hoped that the panel would recommend that I receive a reprimand, a nine-month suspension struck us as a very fair recommendation, and a persuasive one we hoped. We knew, however, that the panel recommendation was just the first step in the process. The second step was review by the full Board of Governors of the Washington State Bar Association, which would determine whether to accept the panel's nine-month suspension recommendation or impose harsher discipline, up to and including disbarment. If the board recommended disbarment, the final decision would be taken to the Supreme Court of Washington State. We understood that it would be several weeks before the Board of Governors reviewed the panel's recommendation, and that if disbarment was recommended, it would be several more months before the Washington Supreme Court heard the case.

My intense desire to be able to practice law was impelled by my realization that I had never really had the chance before I went into government. In law school I had prepared to practice in the growing field of environmental and land use law. Except for the two-month period between passing the bar and joining the Nixon transition team, I had had no law practice experience whatsoever. During my time in government I had gotten to know and respect several highly skilled practicing attorneys. One lawyer in Washington State I admired in particular, James R. Ellis, used his legal skills as an outstanding municipal finance lawyer to support major public improvements in the cleanup of Lake Washington and the construction of dozens of new parks. I had always deeply desired to be able to join men like Ellis at the Washington State bar, and to do so I needed to keep my license to practice.

Following the hearing, Bill and I thanked my friends who at great expense and effort had testified and given me such unstinting support. To this day I feel it was inadequate just to say "thank you" to those who literally put their own careers and reputations on the line on my behalf. They risked a lot in reaching out to help rescue a sinking colleague, and I was then, am now, and will forever be grateful to them.

On August 22, 1974, I flew to Los Angeles, rented a car, and found a room in a motel near Beverly Hills. Up to that point, all of the steps I had taken to accept responsibility and atone for what I had done as head of the Plumbers were in the public arena. But I had not personally apologized to or expressed any remorse directly to Dr. Lewis Fielding, the victim of that crime. I saw that he was not "collateral damage" but an individual person who had been harmed by me. The burglary by the Plumbers of Fielding's office was a direct and personal assault on his property, and the public exposure of the Plumbers' actions had thrust him into the glare of the public spotlight for a while. From what I could tell in reading about him in the press, he was quiet and reserved and prized his privacy. I had concluded that simply pleading guilty to depriving Dr. Fielding of his civil rights and serving a prison sentence was insufficient if I was serious about taking full responsibility for what I had done. The moral debt to him required that I go see him personally and tell him to his face that I was sorry.

As Bill Dwyer had counseled me months before, apologizing to Dr. Fielding was also a step in making amends for what I had done. Taking responsibility is a fundamental value to guide us in making ethical and moral decisions.

I arrived at Dr. Fielding's low-rise office building in Beverly Hills around 1:00 P.M. and went upstairs to his office. It was closed and locked. After waiting in the corridor outside his office for about a half-hour, I wondered whether it would have been a good idea to call and make an appointment. I hadn't called because I wasn't confident that he would agree to see me. But I was so eager to tell him I was sorry that I was willing to risk his displeasure by showing up without an appointment.

A few minutes later I saw him—a slender, bald man with sharp features—walking down the hall. As he approached his office door, I walked over to him and said, "Excuse me, Dr. Fielding, my name is Bud Krogh, and I was wondering if I could speak to you for a few minutes." He looked at me with wide eyes, stepped back, recovered, nodded, and then stuck out his hand to shake my extended hand. "Oh, hello, Mr. Krogh. What did you want to speak to me about?" he said. "Well, sir, I just wanted to come and tell you how sorry I am about what we did to you. It was inexcusable, and I want you to know that."

He looked at me for a moment, inserted the key into the door lock, and said, "Please come in. I have a few minutes before my next appointment." I followed him into his office and at his invitation sat down. He then said, "I'm not surprised you are here. I've read a lot about you." I then told him that I had been released from prison two months earlier and that I had wanted to come see him as soon as I could. I told him that I felt partly responsible for what had happened not only to him but also to the president and his administration. He listened quietly to me, and then told me that he could accept my apology but that I might have additional work ahead to get peace of mind. We talked a short while longer, and then his next appointment arrived and it was time for me to go. He walked me to the door and stuck out his hand. I shook it, thanked him, and we nodded at each other. I felt relieved of a great burden when I walked out of his office and very thankful to him for his kindness, grace, and understanding.

After my meeting with Dr. Fielding, I drove down the coast to San Clemente and got another motel room. Following my request for a time to meet with former President Nixon on August 24, Ron Zeigler, the former White House press secretary and now the top staff person in the San Clemente office, had scheduled me for an hour at 10:00 A.M. The next morning when I drove through the Secret Service security checkpoint on the way to the president's office, I was struck by how quiet and bleak everything felt. When the president vacationed in San Clemente in the past, there had always been a high level of energy, but not that day. When I arrived, it was silent and placid.

The view from the San Clemente office out to the Pacific Ocean was just as spectacular as I remembered it from my previous visits. Just a short three years before I had come to this office to be given the assignment by John Ehrlichman to head up the Special Investigations Unit. I reflected on how much deep and troubled water had flowed under the bridge since then.

When I walked in, the first person I met was Ken Khachigian, one of the savviest political minds on the Nixon staff, and a very good friend. Ken had worked down the hall from me in the Old Executive Office Building, and we had shared many happy experiences. Ken told me that he had signed on to help the president research and write his memoirs. I also saw Diane Sawyer, a former aide to Ron Zeigler in the press office who, like Ken, had joined the San Clemente staff to help with the memoirs. Diane was brilliant and funny. An indefatigable worker, she demonstrated a high degree of personal loyalty to the president by moving to California to work for him. Her successful career in broadcasting since leaving San Clemente is a result of her huge talent and intellect. I then spent a short time with Ron Zeigler, who told me that while the president was functioning well, he was still fragile. Everyone there, including the president, was still numb and in a state of shock. He hoped that I wouldn't be saying anything that would disturb him more. I told him that I just wanted to give him some support and tell him that I was pulling for him. With that, he got up and led me over to the president's office.

The meeting began with Ron Zeigler ushering me into the president's office. We shook hands. He was wearing a dark business suit with an American flag lapel pin. He looked considerably older than I remembered him. His face was flushed, and his eyes were bloodshot. He looked exhausted.

I began by telling him that I was grateful for the chance to see him. I told him that the Washington State Bar Association hearing panel had recommended that I not be disbarred but suspended for a period of nine months. He said he was glad they had only recommended suspension. He said that the California bar was contemplating some action with respect to him, but that he didn't care what they did. "I don't give a damn about that." I said that I felt I had been given a new lease on life and that I was very appreciative of the help so many had given me during the hearing. I noted that men I had known in Washington State as well as in Washington had come to my support.

He asked me, "Do you have any plans now?" I told him that first I was going to return to the District of Columbia for a while. My wife was going to start teaching school around the first week of September, and we had to be back by that time. I said that I hoped to do some teaching. He asked me where. I mentioned that I had been contacted by Paul Hartman, a professor at Florida Technical Institute. He said, "That's a great school. I gave a commencement address there. Great school." I also said that I had been contacted by a person at Indiana University and by someone working with a speakers' program at Mount Holyoke. The latter school was a member of a five-school consortium that shared speakers who came to the campuses. He said, "That's great," when I mentioned that I wanted to do some teaching and seminar work.

I told him that I hoped he knew how proud I was to have served in his administration. I said that I hoped he knew how much good was accomplished. He said, "Well, there were some good things and some bad things." I said, "Yes, that's true, but you can't dwell completely on the bad." He said, "Well, I've said, 'This scandal is the broadest but also the thinnest scandal.'. . . Well, it's all finished now."

In an effort to give him some comfort, I told him that he didn't have to accept that all was finished. I said that I had been very fearful of what might happen to me when the indictments were handed down the previous year. But when I had finally been able to face up directly to what I had done and take responsibility for my actions, I was able to see a course to get through the legal tangle. I also told him that I had seen him come back from hopeless circumstances in the past and that his example had been very helpful to me.

I told him that in prison I had a choice about how I was going to do my time. "Look," I said, "I could have decided to just sit over in a corner of my cell block or just sit against the wall in the prison camp and play my guitar, but I didn't do that. I learned how to plow and tried to be the best plowman I could. I had to learn how to work with my hands. They got cut up. But I learned. I had to take the circumstance as I found it and go from there." He nodded to me as I said these things. I described how I had to see each prisoner there as a man who deserved my respect regardless of what he had done.

He was interrupted by a call from vice presidential nominee Nelson Rockefeller. The president said, "I'm glad they've got you. You've got a lot of clout. . . . No, I'm not just being nice. It's true. . . . I appreciate what you said the other day. Did they give you a hard time about it? Yeah, well, I just don't think it would be good for the country to have a former president dumped in the D.C. jail." There was some more conversation, and then the president said, "Well, good-bye. Give our best to Happy." Then he hung up.

He said that he felt responsible for my actions and asked me whether I thought he should plead guilty. I asked him whether he felt guilty, and he said, "No, I do not." I told him that pleading guilty to a federal crime wasn't a public relations move and that you had to accept that you had committed a crime. I said that there was a line between legal culpability and overall responsibility. I had determined that I was legally responsible and that I had to face it. I said that I appreciated very much his saying that he felt responsible for what had happened. Finally, I said that I wanted him to know that I cared for him very much and wanted to help him in any way I could (as, indeed, I had clearly stated in my letter of resignation to him).

Throughout my conversation with the president, I was mindful of Ron Zeigler's admonition before going in to see him that he was in a fragile state and that I should be careful not to say anything to disturb him further. I was feeling great compassion for the president, so I did not press him on his legal guilt. But when he told me that he did not feel guilty, I knew that he would not be able to acknowledge criminal liability. As he walked me to the door, he put his hand on my shoulder. We shook hands and wished each other well.

Over the next two weeks, I worked on a long memo that laid out in more detail the lessons that I had learned from my experience. I intended to send it to Nixon because I felt that in our conversation I had not been able to go into the detail necessary to explain my reasoning about taking responsibility. The main point I made in that draft memo was that as he worked through these days, he needed to face exactly what had happened. I didn't spell out specifically how he should do this, but I described in detail my own experience as an example. In looking at the evidence against him, it appeared overwhelmingly clear to me that he had obstructed justice on numerous occasions after the Watergate break-in. The evidence amassed against him by the House Judiciary Committee during its impeachment inquiry over an eight-month period was very compelling and had resulted in votes recommending impeachment. More evidence would have been developed by the special prosecutor and grand jury if a case against him had proceeded.

During and right after my meeting with him on August 24, 1974, I felt that if Nixon had been willing to face up to and plead guilty to what he had done as a matter of law, he had it within his grasp to affirm one of the most basic principles in the American legal system—that no man is above the law. I was also confident that if he had taken this path, he would not have been sentenced to a prison where he would have been at risk. But when he answered my question by saying that he did not feel guilty of any crime, it was clear that he felt that either on the facts he had not broken any law or, if he had, the law didn't apply to him because as president he was indeed above the law.

I never sent my memorandum to him because on September 8, 1974, President Gerald Ford "granted . . . a full, free, and absolute pardon unto Richard Nixon for all offenses against the United States which he, Richard Nixon, has committed or may have committed or taken part in during the period from January 20, 1969 through August 9, 1974." Ford's pardon rendered completely moot anything I was going to say in my memo urging the president to face his own legal culpability. He would have the opportunity to face what had happened in writing his memoirs, but such reflection would not be compelled by the threat of any criminal prosecution.

Although Ford's pardon of Nixon could certainly be justified as a humane and compassionate act and as a necessary step to avoid the inevitable national trauma of a protracted investigation and trial, it had the effect of depriving Nixon of the opportunity to face up clearly to what he had done. The pardon was also a major cause of Jimmy Carter's defeat of Gerald Ford in the 1976 election. And at a very basic level, a pardon leaves things unfinished, making it hard to get traction to move forward.

While serving as deputy counsel to the president in 1969, I was occasionally asked to review a high-profile application for presidential clemency that had been submitted to the pardon attorney at the Department of Justice. I became convinced that a pardon or commutation of a prison sentence should be granted only to correct a mistake in a legal process, to serve a humanitarian need, or to acknowledge great service to society in the period after an applicant's release from custody. Because a pardon essentially sets aside the results of a legal process, it should be granted only sparingly.

The year before, I had had to deal with the possibility of a presidential pardon from Richard Nixon. John Ehrlichman told me that in a conversation he had with Nixon after I had resigned from the government, he had pressed the president to offer clemency to me if the need arose. Later in the year, after I decided to plead guilty to the civil rights charge, I had lunch with David Eisenhower at George Washington University. I told him that I felt very strongly that if upon pleading guilty I was sentenced to prison, I did not want any clemency from the president. If a prison sentence was imposed, that was an essential part of taking responsibility for my decision. David told me later that when he was at Camp David with President Nixon and their families, the president decided to grant me a full pardon. David said he reached over to the president—whose hand was on the telephone—and asked him not to do it. "Let Bud work this out in his own way." I was grateful to David for sparing me the embarrassment of having to turn down a presidential pardon if it had been granted.

I felt then, and I do today, that a presidential pardon would have been disastrous for me. Many members of the bar in my home state had expressed grave concern about the negative effect on the reputation of the legal profession of the criminal convictions of so many lawyers in the Watergate scandals. A pardon for me from President Nixon would have exacerbated that sense of betrayal and, I believe, ended any chance of my working as a lawyer again.

After the three-lawyer panel recommended that I be suspended from the practice of law in Washington State for nine months, the jubilation that Bill Dwyer and I had felt was short-lived. Within a few short weeks after the August hearing, the full Board of Governors met in closed session. I testified at length and responded to questions for the better part of a day. After a short review, the board rejected the panel's recommendation for a nine-month suspension and voted to recommend disbarment to the Washington State Supreme Court. Following a hearing before the full court in January 1975, the court issued an opinion in June ordering that I be disbarred. The vote was seven to two in favor of disbarment, with very strong opinions written on both sides. As permitted by court rules, two years later Bill and I applied to the Board of Governors for reinstatement. Again there was a lengthy board hearing, but the board did not support our petition for reinstatement, explaining to us during the closed hearing that not enough time had elapsed from the court's earlier decision to disbar.

We had a decision to make. We were entitled to appeal the board's decision not to support reinstatement to the bar. Bill felt strongly, however, that we needed to take the long-term view and consider the consequences of proceeding to the court without the full support of my professional association. If I wanted to be accepted by my future colleagues at the bar, it would be much better to go forward with the bar association's full support rather than its opposition. Taking the long view was one of the cardinal points that Bill had insisted on when he first took my case in December 1973. We decided not to appeal.

Two years later, in 1979, we again petitioned the Board of Governors for reinstatement, and this time the board concurred. It was a much different setting than the first court hearing in 1975. This second time Kurt Bulmer, another gifted lawyer who had succeeded Michael Jacobsen as bar counsel, argued strongly before the court in favor of my reinstatement. With Bulmer's full support and Bill Dwyer's quiet yet passionate arguments on my behalf, the court heard a powerful case in favor of reinstatement. The court hearing was held in Olympia, Washington, the state capital, about sixty miles south of Seattle. Bill had spent the entire night before at the hospital bedside of his gravely ill mother. During the car drive to Olympia, he was able to rest for about a half-hour. When our case was called, he gave the most eloquent reasons why I should be reinstated. It was a labor of immense dedication and compassion. Four months after the hearing in May 1980, the court voted seven to two to reinstate me, pending my passing the full bar examination. I took the exam in July and was formally sworn in to the practice of law the second time on October 22, 1980.

During the six-year period when I was banished from the practice of law, it was necessary to find a way to support our family. Occasional opportunities to teach and to give lectures on college campuses helped supplement the teacher's salary Suzanne was earning. In the spring of 1975, Congressman Pete McCloskey called me up and invited me down to his office in the Longworth House Office Building. When I walked in, he asked me how things were going.

"Well," I answered, "I'm not waiting beside the phone hoping that the White House will call and offer me a job." He laughed and asked if I would ever consider working with the legislative branch. "Yes, sir," I answered. He chuckled and then asked if I would consider working for the House of Representatives. "Yes, sir," I answered again, wondering where this was going. "Bud, would you consider working for me?" I was overwhelmed. "Absolutely, I would. It would be a great privilege!"

He led me into the adjoining office where his administrative assistant and public information staff member had their desks. He pointed to a vacant desk with a lone file on top in the corner. "There's your desk. Fill out the forms in the file, and then let's go downstairs and get you a pass."

So began another federal job for a man I deeply respected and admired. Some people rescue dogs and cats. McCloskey rescued people. During the time I worked with him I heard many stories about people who had fallen on hard times and subsequently been helped by the congressman. Hiring me at a time when the Watergate debacle was still a fresh wound in the minds of most Americans took tremendous moral courage. He was a physically courageous fighting marine during the Korean War, and he was a morally courageous public servant throughout his terms in the Congress. He was also brilliant, funny, and irreverent. The inscription to me in his gripping book *The Taking of Hill 610* reads: "To Egil 'Himself' Krogh, the most honest scoundrel I know, Pete McCloskey."

For the next eight months I worked on McCloskey's staff in Washington, D.C., and back in his district in Palo Alto, California. My areas of responsibility included merchant marine matters, Russian competition in shipping, and transportation bottlenecks in McCloskey's district. It was interesting work, but I soon felt that it was time to try something completely new. During one of the periods I worked in the Palo Alto office, I fell in love with the Bay Area and decided it was time to leave Washington, D.C., and move to San Francisco. This decision followed my disbarment in May 1975, when I realized that it would be a long time before I could return to the practice of law in Washington State. So in late 1975 I moved to San Francisco to begin a new life on my own. After a year in business, an opportunity to make amends to a wider cross-section of society presented itself almost immediately.

A close friend of mine, Tom Fletcher, had been serving as the deputy mayor of Washington, D.C., during my first two years on the White House staff. Tom was an experienced, no-nonsense professional manager, and as the president's liaison with the District government, I had come to rely heavily on his judgment. When he left Washington for a position at Stanford Research Institute, we stayed in touch. I had told him of my decision to move to San Francisco.

One day he called and asked me to have lunch with him and a close friend of his, Dr. Randy Hamilton, who was the dean of the Graduate School of Public Administration at Golden Gate University. We met for lunch at the grand old Palace Hotel on the corner of Montgomery and Market Streets. Dr. Hamilton was a droll, sprightly genius who regaled Tom and me with stories of his long and illustrious academic career. As we discussed some of my work in Washington, D.C., Dr. Hamilton turned to Tom and said, "Bud is going to teach one of our sections on public policy analysis next quarter." Tom and I looked at each other very confused. This was the first we had heard about it. "I am?" I answered, looking uncertain. "Absolutely. You'll be great. First rate. Is this okay with you?" "Yes, sir," I answered. "This will be great."

So began my new career of teaching public administration to graduate students at Golden Gate University. I found this profession deeply satisfying. The work I enjoyed the most on the White House staff was converting public policy concepts into real, effective programs and designing the legislative, organizational, and budgetary systems that would implement those concepts. I had had real-life experience in the world of public administration, and the focus of the Golden Gate University approach was the practical application of sound theory. For the next four and a half years, I taught public policy analysis, introductory public administration, values and conflicts in public management, and administrative law.

In the spring of 1976, I was teaching public policy analysis and one of the sections of the course covered foreign policy. It had been almost two years since I had last seen Richard Nixon in San Clemente right after his resignation. In that period he had weathered a near-fatal bout of phlebitis. After recovering, he had been hard at work writing his memoirs. I called his office and asked if

I could meet with him to get some insight into how best to present this section of the course.

On April 23, 1976, I met with Nixon from 11:45 A.M. to 1:10 P.M. He looked tanned, rested, and in good spirits. His eyes were clear and focused. He had long since recovered from the devastation of his resignation twenty months before. I thanked him for seeing me and told him that as I had mentioned to him at our earlier meeting, I was now teaching at the graduate level. I told him my focus in the course I was teaching was on the theory behind his foreign policy, the attitudes he felt a leader must express in order to implement policy successfully, and the mechanisms that must be put in place. I mentioned that I would be discussing the international narcotics program for which I had had responsibility in the White House, but that I needed some understanding of how the other major elements of our foreign policy were approached.

He said, "You must have idealism and good public relations; but you also must have tough, even ruthless pragmatism to back it up." He stressed that a leader must understand the issues thoroughly. He said that in the area of foreign policy, he had traveled to every country; he understood how other leaders thought, and he felt that this was where his major contribution would be.

In a wide-ranging monologue, he gave me a highly animated seminar on China, Russia, the Middle East, Henry Kissinger, the National Security Council, and secrecy. When he went to China, he did not start out with Mao by saying what a great moment this was and how terrific their meeting was. He started out by saying that he believed in the American system and he knew that Mao believed in his system. He wasn't there saying that he had changed his mind about anything. Mao responded by saying that "history" had brought them together. Nixon said to me that by this Mao meant that necessity was responsible for the meeting. Nixon said that when you are dealing with other nations, "it is important to keep in mind that the other country is always dealing from its own interest. This is the point that has to be appreciated."

The Soviet Union did not recoil from the United States after our initiative to China. This was what some had expected. Rather, the Soviets recognized the need not to have a China-U.S. combination that could endanger their country. So in this case, too, Soviet interest dictated its response to the United States, and the moves toward détente could begin. What is of importance to understand in both examples is the long view each nation was taking. The issues were ones of survival, which is a nation's most fundamental self-interest.

On the Middle East, Nixon recounted a meeting he had had with some American supporters of Israel. He asked them whether they would like to have an America that was a friend of Israel only or an America that was a friend of Israel as well as a friend of the Arabs. They responded that they wanted an America that was a friend of Israel only.

Nixon told them that this might well have been shortsighted of them. If the United States had no relations with the Arabs, a vacuum would be created. And while the Egyptians and the Syrians had no love for the Russians, there was no other country but Russia to which the Arab world could turn for its hardware. Nixon felt that it was in Israel's long-term interest and security for the United States to establish closer relations with the Arab world and begin discussions leading to working relationships. It wouldn't take 100 million Arabs forever to really learn how to fight, he pointed out, and then Israel would surely suffer for it.

When he mentioned Henry Kissinger, he gave me a thin smile. Nixon said that Kissinger was a brilliant tactician and negotiator who needed the backup of a strong leader who would keep him on course. Nixon said that he himself had achieved his understanding of the world from experience, from his travels, and from his meetings with various heads of state, and not so much from reading the many papers on the subject, as clearly Kissinger had done.

Nixon used his National Security Council to get a broad range of options. He had instructed Kissinger to appoint both hawks and doves to the council to ensure that he was given all points of view on a subject. He did not ask for a show of hands. Once he had a full range of views, he would ponder them, perhaps discuss them with Kissinger, and then make his decision. He would stay with his decision until changed circumstances dictated otherwise.

On secrecy, Nixon mentioned that he had always been an admirer of Woodrow Wilson and agreed with his vision of "open covenants, openly arrived at." But when we were dealing with enemies, such as China and Russia, security was mandatory for successful diplomacy. This was so because those countries had excellent security and expected it of us. Without it, no diplomacy would be undertaken. With regard to his initiative to China, the State Department was not told about it, and Secretary Rogers did not know until three days before. Secretary of Defense Melvin Laird was never told about it because he would surely have leaked it.

As in his earlier monologue to the students at the Lincoln Memorial in 1970, Nixon was able to cover a wide range of subjects with clarity and focus. There was no doubt in my mind that he had the broadest understanding of how the world actually worked and that he was proud of his achievements. As he spoke, I felt that he would have made an outstanding professor. He was perhaps beginning to see a role for himself as a respected elder statesman emerging from the rubble of his political career. I felt that he wanted me to understand his vision so that I could pass it on to my students and share it through the rest of my career. His ideas helped me to add in-depth knowledge, balance, and perspective to the courses I was teaching on public policy and ethics in public administration.

I thanked Nixon for his time. I think he felt some obligation to help me in my new teaching career, and I was grateful for that.

In reviewing and typing up the notes from our meeting, I realized that he had given me some fairly basic ideas. Perhaps the comment that most illuminated his approach to policy, and to government and politics generally, was his statement of the need for idealism and good public relations backed up with a "ruthless pragmatism." In my experience with him, he was clearly results-oriented, and he was not hung up on any ideology that might conflict with what he felt was a reasonable, practical result. He seemed also to be more oriented to understanding the fundamental interests that drove the actions of foreign leaders rather than interested in their personalities.

For the next two years I taught full-time at Golden Gate University, usually teaching courses at night. I lived in the town of Mill Valley, five miles north of the Golden Gate Bridge in Marin County. By day I would read books and run on Mount Tamalpais to keep fit. As a refugee from the Watergate wars, I found this to be a time of recovery and reflection.

Bill Dwyer continued to prepare the ground for our hearings in Washington State on reinstatement to the bar. We had been very grateful for the support that Leon Jaworski, the Watergate special prosecutor, had given to our cause in the two hearings before the three-lawyer panel and the Board of Governors. He had written letters arguing strongly that I was fit to practice law and urging that I be allowed back into the bar as soon as possible.

On October 16, 1978, Jaworski was to give a lecture on morality in government at the University of California at Berkeley in

Wheeler Auditorium. The main course I was teaching that quarter at Golden Gate University was one in values and conflicts in public management for about twenty doctoral degree students. His subject and the course content fit perfectly, so I felt that it would be a good experience for them to hear him.

When we arrived, the auditorium was packed. We were able to find seats together for the class on the far right side of the hall. Over seven hundred students, faculty, and assorted Berkeley activists were jammed into the hall. I wanted to see if I could visit briefly with Jaworski afterwards to thank him for his support. So I wrote a note telling him that I was there with my class and asking if I could see him later. I walked up to the stage and handed it to a woman who appeared to be in charge. What happened over the next hour and a half painted an indelible memory for me as my emotions ranged from stark terror to humble gratitude.

Jaworski's own account appears in the epilogue to his book *Confession and Avoidance*:

As I walked into the auditorium, wedging my way through the students, one of my hosts handed me a note. I put the paper in my coat pocket and read it after I had taken my seat on the stage.

The message was from the first White House aide to be indicted, and sentenced to prison, as a result of the Watergate crimes. He had lost his license to practice law and now taught a class in public administration at the university. His note, scrawled in black ink on a small square of memo paper, said he was in the audience with his students. He would like to say hello after my talk. He would understand if we could not.

I was surprised, and pleased, and struck by more than a touch of irony. The topic of my speech was "Morality in Government." Even as I stood at the microphone, listening to my words echo in the quiet, my mind wandered to the note in my pocket and the man who wrote it. I was not sure what I would do, or even what I wanted to do.

As I moved deeper into the points on Watergate, I instinctively stopped and departed from the text. I said, "One of the men who was involved in this case is in our audience tonight. His experience in government goes to the heart of this issue and what we can learn from it. I must tell you that I have a high regard for him today. He is a man who acknowledged his mistake and paid a price for it. What is more, he asked for no favors or special privileges, from the prosecutor or the court. He said he found his own conduct indefensible and he was willing to take the punishment for what he had done.

"I admire him," I went on, "for the manner in which he accepted the responsibility for his actions. I cannot say the same for his former employer, his President."

As I paused, to look down at my speech and find my place, I was aware of a murmuring in the crowd. Later, in the question and answer period, a student rose and asked, "Sir, would you mind identifying the individual to whom you made reference during your Watergate comments?"

I said, "No I will not. That would be an invasion of his privacy for me to single him out. He is here as a member of this audience, as you are." I looked around the room. "However, if he does not object to making his presence known, I would leave it to him to do so. If he is willing to be recognized, this would be an appropriate time."

Heads turned and craned. Time seemed to freeze as I waited. I did not even know if he was still in the room, or where he was seated.

Then, off to my left, there was a stir. Not in a bouncy, proud way, but slowly, with some reluctance, he climbed to his feet and looked around uncertainly.

I nodded, made a quick gesture with my left hand and said, "This is Egil (Bud) Krogh."

The auditorium vibrated with applause, a sound that swelled and grew and slapped off the walls. The ovation must have lasted two or three minutes. I do not know how many political rallies I have attended, although the number is too many, but I have never seen or heard anything quite as genuine as the emotion that crowd gave to Bud Krogh, an ex-lawyer who had just been introduced by the man who sent him to prison. . . .

. . . After the program ended, and I stood chatting at the podium and even signing autographs, Bud Krogh appeared at my side. All we said was hello, but we shook hands and our eyes caught and, at that moment, I felt a flicker of hope. The enduring question of Watergate is whether we, as a people, will learn from it. Some have.

When Jaworski indicated during his speech that now would be a good time for me to be recognized, I was struck with terror. Here I was, with my class, at the epicenter of the radical movement in America. I didn't believe there was one person in that hall who had voted for Richard Nixon. Would I be attacked? I looked over at my students, who were glancing at me with worried faces. One of them pointed to a side exit we could use if we had to escape quickly. But I felt too that not to acknowledge Jaworski's gracious offer to recognize me would be rude and cowardly. So I got up, very slowly so that I could gauge how bad things could get. I was dumbfounded by the overwhelming applause that erupted, and I must attribute most of it to the high respect that audience felt for Jaworski.

In discussing this experience later with my students, we acknowledged how important it is to own up to our mistakes and not try to blame others for our own errors. This was a theme I emphasized in the courses I taught over the next two years before returning to Seattle. Again and again, the importance of taking responsibility for one's actions emerged as a vital life principle.

Bill Dwyer and I were finally successful. After reinstatement to the Washington bar on October 22, 1980, I joined Bill Dwyer's law firm in Seattle. I practiced law at Culp, Dwyer, Guterson & Grader for the next fifteen years before going out on my own as a lawyer. For the first time since 1968—when I left Seattle for Washington, D.C.—I had returned home to my place, my profession, and a semblance of stability.

CHAPTER 13

An Open Letter to the Bush Administration

O ver the next twenty years I lived a fairly quiet life, focus-
ing on developing my mediation and energy law practices. I indulged my passion for mountain climbing by
helping to organize Project Pelion, a climb of Mount Rainier by
courageous disabled climbers, and the 1990 Mount Everest Earth
Day International Peace Climb, which brought together a team
of climbers from the Soviet Union, China, and the United States
for a successful climb of Mount Everest. But for the most part, I
lived a private life and gave only a few talks on my former government work here and there.

After the 2000 election, however, I felt impelled to speak out.
I was sitting at home watching the news on January 28, 2001.
One of the first stories showed the newly minted Bush staff being
sworn in by the chief justice in the East Room of the White
House. Except for the president and his most senior advisers,
they all looked young and eager and innocent. Three of his senior advisers—Vice President Cheney, Secretary of the Treasury
Paul O'Neill, and Secretary of Defense Donald Rumsfeld—were
men I had worked with on the Nixon staff. I felt a real connection

to the younger Bush staff members as they were sworn in. I knew they were going to be on a much larger and more precarious stage than they had ever performed on before.

Watching them raise their right hands and swear to uphold the Constitution brought back a flood of memories from when I was sworn in thirty-two years before as a new member of President Nixon's White House staff. It was almost a lifetime ago; I had been sworn in as a twenty-nine-year-old. I remembered the great sense of awe and solemn responsibility that I had felt. And I recalled how humbled I felt by being given the privilege of serving the president and the opportunity to do something worthwhile for the country.

When President Nixon spoke to us and the media after we were sworn in, he was very gracious to our families and friends. He told everyone, "These are the men and women who will be working long hours in the White House and in the Executive Office Building and who will be away from their families a great deal. That is one of the reasons we invited the families. We want you to take a good look at them. You may not see too much of them later."

I remembered that the president was good to his word. Most everyone on the Nixon staff worked incredibly long hours, and we didn't see very much of our families. In my home, I always left for work long before our boys woke up and arrived home long after they were asleep. White House staff work was punctuated by many exciting and thrilling moments, and I never worked so hard for so long as I did on Nixon's staff.

As I pondered what the new Bush staff would encounter, I realized that I might be able to help by writing a memo to them about one of the central ideas that I had not understood as well as I should have when I was on the White House staff. That central idea was and is the absolute imperative to maintain one's sense of integrity in the face of enormous pressures to get results at any cost.

Since leaving Washington, D.C., in 1975, I had occasionally glanced at the formal commissions that had appointed me to the various governmental positions I held. I received four commissions over the course of four and a half years: deputy counsel to the president, deputy assistant to the president for domestic affairs, associate director of the Domestic Council, and undersecretary of the Department of Transportation. The appointment clause of each commission began with similar words: "Reposing special trust in the integrity . . . of [your name]," the president appoints you to your position. The key point that I had not thoroughly internalized was that the integrity in which the president was reposing special trust was my own. Not his integrity, not the integrity of someone else on the staff, but my own. In short, no one can check their personal integrity at the door when they walk into work at the West Wing or anywhere else.

I had come to the view that some of us on the Nixon White House staff had succumbed to a horrendous meltdown of our personal integrity in some of the decisions we had made. This breakdown in integrity had contributed to the eventual sinking of the president's ship of state. To counter this slippery slope for others in government and business, I had been developing an approach for staying in a zone of integrity where one can perform one's job safely and successfully. This approach involved asking and honestly answering two key questions: Is it whole and complete? And is it right?

Over the years since I served on the White House staff, I had seen politics and public life in Washington, D.C., becoming meaner and more contentious. There seemed to be a breakdown in civility. I felt increasingly that the best way to avoid attacks was simply to do one's work with the highest degree of integrity. To help the new Bush staff members avoid getting ensnared in painful circumstances later, I immediately started drafting a memo to them.

I felt that the best forum for such a memo was the *Christian Science Monitor* because of its stated purpose: "To injure no man, but to bless all mankind." The *Monitor* also had an excellent reputation as an unbiased international daily newspaper. In the memo, I explained how the actions of the White House Plumbers represented a major breakdown of integrity. One of the most critical points in the memo was the need for the lawyers on the president's staff to constantly ask the question: is it legal? I remembered that during my work as codirector of the Plumbers, I had assumed that because the president described our assignment as critical to national security, we could carry out a covert operation with impunity. The president was, after all, the commander in chief, and to the extent that we thought about it at all, this constitutional power gave us (as agents of the president) sufficient authority for carrying out an operation that might otherwise be illegal under domestic criminal law.

Sooner or later I felt that the Bush White House would encounter a serious national security threat. This belief was not based on any evidence that President George W. Bush would be more likely than any other president to encounter a national security threat. It is simply a fact that most presidents have faced such threats on their watch. So I strongly urged in the memo that the lawyers on the staff get prepared for such a contingency and not allow themselves to be so swept up in the urgency of a crisis that they would be tempted to abandon their integrity-based legal and analytical skills. "National security" and "commander in chief" were terms that the Plumbers never explored deeply, and as a result they made some terribly bad decisions. I urged the Bush lawyers to make sure in their work for the new administration that these terms were well researched and that their legal advice was based on established precedent.

I wrote in the memo:

> While it seems obvious, it is also crucial to ask, "Is it legal?"
> White House lawyers need to ask this question a lot and be able
> to answer it affirmatively. In formulating your answers, I recommend that you use interpretations of the law that are well established in statute and precedent, and do not rely on hazy,
> loose definitions of what you think words like "national security," "commander-in-chief," "trust fund," and the like might be
> tortured into meaning. It will help you lawyers, too, to be constantly vigilant to any violation of the Bill of Rights.

I felt when writing the memo that White House lawyers could face future pressure to come up with strained interpretations of the law to justify and give legal cover to what the president might want to do.

The *Monitor* published this memorandum to the Bush staff on February 12, 2001. Seven months later, Al Qaeda terrorists flew planes into the World Trade Center and the Pentagon. The president announced almost immediately that the United States was at war and began to exercise (with the concurrence of Congress) the broad range of powers that wartime commanders in chief demand.

One of America's great historians, David McCullough, observed recently that the powers exercised by a president during periods of national security crisis have, like a pendulum, swung back and forth throughout our history. As threats become more immediate and severe, presidents unilaterally claim and exercise expansive powers to respond to those threats. McCullough gave as examples President Lincoln's suspension of the writ of habeas corpus during the Civil War and President Franklin Roosevelt's approval of exclusion orders during World War II when American citizens of Japanese extraction were rounded up and consigned to camps away from their homes for the duration of the war.

In times of extreme threat there is obvious risk of overreaching in the legitimate exercise of presidential power. The decision of the Plumbers in the Nixon White House to carry out a covert operation was not only an obvious overreach and flagrant abuse of the president's article 2 power as commander in chief but also a serious crime under U.S. law.

Over the past several years, the Bush administration has systematically taken steps to expand the power of the president to attack the terrorist threat and keep America safe. There is no question that a fundamental responsibility of the president and the executive branch is to maintain order, to ensure the domestic tranquillity, and to keep America safe. But during the past few years since writing the memo for the *Monitor*, I have been disappointed to observe the Bush administration take a number of actions that appear to exceed generally accepted views of the lawful and constitutional scope of the president's powers.

A specific example of such an action is the secret surveillance program that was initiated in 2001 and that authorized and directed the National Security Agency (NSA) to intercept without a warrant the international phone calls of numerous people and organizations within the United States with individuals abroad who are suspected of ties to terrorists. When the program became publicly known through an article by James Risen and Eric Lichtblau in the *New York Times* on December 16, 2005, there was an eruption of anger from those who felt that the president had unilaterally decided to strip away from thousands of citizens their fundamental constitutional rights to privacy.

It is not surprising that the Bush administration reacted with anger at the public disclosure of the program and launched an attack on the patriotism of those who revealed such a vital state secret. The reaction was similar to the rage that President Nixon had expressed upon the release of the Pentagon Papers and the fallback position of the United States in the SALT 1 talks. Moreover, the same national security justification that the Plumbers used to justify the covert operation in the Pentagon Papers case in 1971 was used to justify the initiation of the NSA surveillance program in 2001.

Legal challenges to the NSA surveillance program followed immediately after its disclosure. The heart of these challenges is that the surveillance program violates the constitutional rights of those citizens whose conversations are intercepted by the NSA. Specifically, those bringing suit have alleged that the free speech and association rights of U.S. citizens under the First Amendment and their privacy rights under the Fourth Amendment have been violated. They also allege that the surveillance program violates the principle of separation of powers because the president has exceeded his authority under article 2 of the Constitution. A final argument is that the program violates the statutory limits placed on such intercepts by the Foreign Intelligence Surveillance Act (FISA).

The Bush administration has defended its conduct by asserting that the president as commander in chief has the inherent power to authorize and direct such surveillance. It has also claimed that the FISA provisions are too cumbersome and were designed for a different period when there was not so great a need to intercept conversations instantaneously. Adopted in the aftermath of the abuses of Watergate and the Plumbers' activities in which I was involved, FISA sets out express requirements for getting authorization from a special court to wiretap individuals.

None of the FISA provisions were followed by the NSA in the surveillance program ordered by President Bush.

On August 17, 2006, Anna Diggs Taylor, a U.S. District Court judge in Michigan, ruled that the NSA surveillance program violated the First and Fourth Amendments, the separation of powers principle, and the FISA statute. Immediately after the ruling, the president, surrounded by his national security team at Camp David, castigated the decision of the District Court, pledged an immediate appeal, and predicted a reversal.

On a broader scale, the similarity is striking between the claim of almost limitless presidential power as stated by President Nixon in an interview with David Frost ("When the president does it, it's not illegal") and the claim by President Bush that the NSA surveillance program is consistent with the Constitution and statutory law. If the lower court's ruling on the NSA program is upheld on appeal, then another blow will have been struck for the vital proposition that no man, including no president, is above the law.

Another egregious example of the Bush administration's willingness to twist legality in its favor was the preparation and issuance in 2002 of a legal memorandum that has proven to be flagrantly flawed, wrong, and lacking in basic integrity of analysis. Specifically, a memorandum written primarily by John Yoo in the Office of Legal Counsel in the Department of Justice on the question of torture (known as the "Bybee Memorandum") was deeply disturbing. This analysis asserted extreme positions on the definition of torture and the expansive powers of the president as commander in chief.

If this memorandum had been simply an argument in a brief to a court, where advocacy of a position sometimes features a degree of exaggeration of the merits of that position and where the decider of the issue is the court, there would be less concern about the extreme nature of the positions asserted. But the memorandum was intended to essentially create law, not interpret or follow it. In so doing, the memorandum "tortured" the meaning of "torture" and "commander in chief" to justify the interrogation protocols that the Defense Department intended to implement in the prisons at Guantanamo Bay and Abu Ghraib.

When the memorandum became public, the negative reaction from most leading constitutional scholars about its unsoundness led to its withdrawal a short two years after it was issued. But extreme harm had already been done by those who had been entrusted with administering the prisons in Guantanamo Bay and Abu Ghraib and who were partially relying upon the memo. The excessive force, degradation, cruelty, and humiliation inflicted on prisoners in U.S. custody at Abu Ghraib and Guantanamo Bay wounded America's reputation for decency and integrity and has contributed in some measure to the ongoing anger and hatred aimed at the United States in the Muslim world.

These many examples of loss of integrity have made me particularly concerned about the condition of public life in the United States. In a country like America, where the rule of law is supposed to be paramount, we have to be able to believe in the integrity of our public officials, civil servants, business leaders, and neighbors. Without this respect for each other and our underlying beliefs, without a commitment to living and acting with integrity, we can only expect more of the same problems, with good people placed in circumstances where bad decisions become all but unavoidable.

CHAPTER 14

Integrity in
Public Life

F rom the moment I decided to plead guilty to my crime, the issues of conscience and integrity have been foremost in my mind. It has not been easy to make the decision to "go public" with my thoughts on integrity and public life, on my time in the White House, and on what has happened since. One particular idea has pushed me forward: the demise of the Nixon administration should have been a cautionary tale for anyone in the public sphere, but so far those lessons haven't been heard.

So many of us entered public service with a belief that we would personally be able to change things for the better. When we joined Nixon's administration, there was every possibility that our work would be fully beneficial, both for the current state of affairs and for the long term. Nixon had some enlightened policies that even today would seem cutting-edge—in particular, his treatment-oriented drug programs, which were developed because of his ability to listen to reason and the conclusions of experts and staffers. But it was in this environment of trying to change things for the better that we, his staffers, failed him and, at the same time, Nixon failed us and the American people.

Outside pressures had a strong influence on my decisions while I was a Nixon staffer, but there were strong internal threats as well. From my parents' and the Navy's influences, I had been raised as a patriot and a believer in the paramount importance of national defense. Nixon and Ehrlichman both knew this. When they were looking for a zealot—in their words, someone like Nixon himself—they were able to find in me a quintessential team player whose belief in the importance of the security issues was enough to drive him over the line. My willingness to believe wholeheartedly in the judgment of President Nixon and John Ehrlichman—a manifestation of unbalanced loyalties—nullified any ability I might have had to question their instructions.

There was also a degree of hubris and vanity in my decision making, as Judge Gesell pointed out. Rarely during my White House career did I ask the question, "Can I do this?" Whether because of my youth or my naïveté, I felt confident that I could perform whatever was assigned to me and rarely questioned my abilities. But a simple fact remained—I did not have the experience or skills to direct a secret intelligence operation.

My willingness to take the job was also a product of ambition. I had gone to the White House with Ehrlichman after only one second of consideration. "Do you want to go?" he asked me. "Yes, sir!" I answered. I wanted to do the right thing both by my president and by my career, and when assigned to the SIU, I was unwilling to suffer the professional consequences of refusing to take the actions that the president so clearly wanted.

I was also somewhat overwhelmed. During that intense period in 1971 when I was preoccupied with international narcotics problems, I was simply unable to devote the time and energy necessary to make sure everything in the SIU operation went smoothly. There just wasn't time to step back and fully consider the potential dangers and risks my decisions posed. A healthy sign of high-level competence can be found in the high-risk actions you choose not to pursue. Unfortunately, I didn't recognize these risks until after the fact, when I saw pictures of the destruction of Dr. Fielding's office and Liddy let me know that he had treated the covert operation as a matter of life or death.

As I look back on that period in 1971, I am struck by how much history would have been different if I could have stepped out of the Plumbers' cocoon and asked a few questions of my colleagues. One simple question to my friend John Dean could have made all the difference. In a recent talk on a national tour to promote his new book, *Conservatives Without Conscience*, I heard Dean recount the story of how he risked professional banishment by forcefully opposing and getting canceled the president's order to burglarize the Brookings Institution to get the Pentagon Papers. He immediately understood the unlawfulness and the insanity of the president's order to burglarize the Brookings Institution. Perhaps after one conversation with Dean at that crucial moment in 1971, the Plumbers might have never been assembled. Room 16 would have remained a scarcely used administrative office on the way to the mail room. Dr. Fielding would have remained a private citizen. And Richard Nixon, an emotional, volatile, patriotic politician might today be regarded as one of the greats, not one of the great lapses, of American political history.

These experiences, followed today by a failure to learn the lessons of the past, show a clear need for a concept that allows an independent, moral thinker to feel assured that he or she is making the best choice in a specific set of circumstances. In trying to clarify that concept, I have continually wrestled with my conscience and with what the definition of integrity really means and requires from us. In *Webster's Dictionary*, *integrity* is defined as:

1. adherence to moral and ethical principles; soundness of moral character; honest
2. the state of being whole, entire, undiminished: to preserve the integrity of the empire
3. a sound, unimpaired, or perfect condition: the integrity of a ship's hull

Synonyms. 1. rectitude, probity, virtue

Most people think of the first definition as the main meaning of integrity, but when I reasoned through the importance of integrity, the second and third definitions seemed useful as well. When you try to think through a choice, what do you do? You look at the facts on the ground, and preferably *all* of the facts. You need to understand how those facts—people, things, events—are interrelated. You examine the whole system and the context in which you are making a decision. To evaluate all that analysis you've done, you need to ask yourself, "Is my decision whole and complete?"

No matter what activity we are engaged in, there is a surrounding field or context for our decisions. How many times have you wondered if you're seeing the whole picture? When people make bad decisions, the criticisms you usually hear are on the order of: "She just didn't get it," "Should've looked before he leapt," and "What could they have been thinking?" All too often we just don't stop, take a step back from an important decision, and try to understand the whole picture. Making sure that you do step back and take this view is the core idea of the question: is it whole and complete?

In addition, just because your choice makes sense intellectually doesn't mean it's the right thing to do. Whatever you choose to do will always directly affect people, the situation, or your own life. When you look at those effects, it is crucial that you bring your moral sense to bear on what you are doing.

It's especially important to ask the question: is it right? The rightness of our actions never seemed relevant to the Plumbers when we decided to break into Dr. Fielding's office to examine his files on Daniel Ellsberg. We asked ourselves operational questions such as: Who has the skills to carry out this covert operation? Can they be trusted? How can we assure ourselves that nothing can be traced back to the White House? Who should pay for it? Will the CIA provide logistical support? We just assumed we were right because the president was pressing for action and we were working on his behalf.

If we had asked ourselves about the rightness of our actions, we would at least have considered their direct impacts on Dr. Fielding. We would have asked whether it was moral and just to strip away an American citizen's right to be free from an unwarranted search of his office. We might have asked whether national security can ever justify actions that contradict a nation's core values—what sort of security is that, and what price is being paid for it, if it undermines the character of the state it is supposed to secure? But those questions were not asked, at least not by me, until my trip to Williamsburg two years too late.

All too often the question isn't about right versus wrong but about the much more difficult choice between two apparently right answers. I have found the work of Rushworth Kidder and the Institute for Global Ethics to be particularly useful in coming to grips with "right versus right" dilemmas. In his book *How Good People Make Tough Choices*, Kidder writes that there are four "right versus right" paradigms:

1. Truth versus loyalty
2. Short-term versus long-term
3. Justice versus mercy
4. Self versus community

Applying the first two paradigms to the conduct of the White House Plumbers, it can be seen immediately that loyalty and short-term reasoning were dominating the deliberations of that group. These paradigms help clarify what is influencing decisions. To assist in making decisions that are closest to the highest right, Kidder then offers three resolution approaches. The first is ends-based: what is the greatest good for the greatest number? The second is rule-based: should this approach be a universal rule for all? The third approach is care-based and derived from the Golden Rule: would I want this decision to apply to me? The Plumbers' national security justification might arguably have fit the first resolution approach, but it failed the next two.

My ability to think clearly about how to resolve competing values was enhanced by taking one of the ethical fitness seminars offered by Kidder's Institute for Global Ethics (www.globalethics .org). Lee Marrella's book *In Search of Ethics* also provides helpful guidance on how to live an ethical, value-based life and contains in-depth stories about and interviews with many individuals who reflect the highest moral principles in their lives.

The direct effects of our actions are what we most often think of when we ask, is it right? But there is a third meaning of the word *integrity* buried at the bottom of the dictionary definition, along with the synonyms "rectitude, probity, virtue." I think a reasonable summary of the meanings of those words is "good."

When we look at our actions and their impacts, we may think it's simplistic to ask, is it good? But answering the question can be quite complex. Immediately upon asking ourselves about the goodness of our decision, a half-dozen other questions spring to mind. Who benefits from this decision? Will this decision promote harmony? Decrease suffering? Enhance peace? Are we drawing from the best qualities and motivations within us in making this decision? Does this decision reflect our highest understanding of the truth? Most of all, the important thing to understand is this: *any of the world's great spiritual traditions can help us understand what is good, but personal integrity will still be the guide to our actions.*

Dr. David Hawkins, one of the great thinkers and spiritual sages of our time, has helped me to understand this truth: that integrity and understanding what is good are linked. In his writings, he charts out and calibrates the range of human consciousness from the lowest to the highest levels. Within this range, he shows how integrity forms the basis for all the higher levels above it.

The lowest level starts with shame and moves up through guilt, apathy, hatred, grief, fear, desire, anger, and pride. These lower levels he defines as the levels of falsehood where force is the energy for getting things done.

As he progresses up the scale of human consciousness, the level of integrity is identified as the break point between the lower levels and the higher levels. The higher levels, starting from integrity, move upward to courage, neutrality, willingness, acceptance, reason, love, joy, peace, and enlightenment. Above the integrity break point are the increasing levels of truth where true power based on moral and spiritual energy is the driver for getting things done.

I believe that Dr. Hawkins is exactly right in identifying integrity as the essential characteristic of consciousness, without which life cannot be lived truthfully and with purpose, meaning, satisfaction, and grace. Below the level of integrity, decisions are often faulty, and life is lived without much assurance of meaning, purpose, assurance, or peace. The lower levels of consciousness lead to the state of nature pictured by the great British natural law thinker Thomas Hobbes, who saw life before any civil state or rule of law as "solitary, poor, nasty, brutish, and short" (*Leviathan*, 1651).

Hawkins offers a methodology for testing the consciousness level of just about anything. In applying his analysis of consciousness levels to my experience on Nixon's staff, there is a clear correlation between some of the lower levels that drove some of the Plumbers—hatred, anger, and pride—and the disastrous decision to break into the office of Dr. Lewis Fielding. That covert action was an application of pure force outside the rule of law, not an exercise of the real power that Hawkins maintains derives from moral and spiritual values. And it led to my falsehood in testimony before a U.S. attorney. If we had understood that integrity was the level of consciousness that was critical to our success, we might have had the courage to think through the consequences of our actions and to allow reason and morality to guide our thought and conduct. As I understand Dr. Hawkins's thesis, integrity and the levels of consciousness above it are not just "nice to have" qualities of mind. They are essential states of consciousness that determine our very survival.

Stories about the apparent breakdowns in integrity of members of the Bush administration continue to rivet our attention. However, there also appears to be a wider, more systemic breakdown in ethical conduct in many of our institutions, whether government, business, sports, academia, or the media. A chilling book by David Callahan entitled *The Cheating Culture: Why More Americans Are Doing Wrong to Get Ahead* identifies the drive to win at all costs in the competitive open market as a principal reason for unethical behavior. He is right: when success is determined only by whether one has won or lost, rather than by the positive impacts of one's activities, then unethical behavior is a clear consequence. Many who compete in these markets feel that cheating is acceptable and necessary so as not to lose out on opportunities.

A recent article by David Francis in the *Christian Science Monitor* laid out a litany of corporate crimes that seem to increase every day. This increase in corrupt practices he describes as the "Gross Corruption Product." Helping to bolster Francis's "GCP," the Enron debacle still commands headlines as prison sentences are handed out and the civil litigation to extract more funds from participating banks continues. Sports has seen an epidemic of steroid use, perhaps the epitome of the win-at-all-costs mentality, especially when we start to see athletes sacrificing their health and even their lives by taking performance-enhancing drugs.

Of course, the win-at-all-costs mentality can be seen at all levels of business. Long sentences imposed on corporate leaders are daily staples in the press. In late 2006, major news stories recounted how the board chairperson at one Fortune 500 company, Patricia Dunn of Hewlett-Packard, authorized a potentially unlawful investigation to secure information about leaks from other members of the board. I followed this story with keen interest and asked myself why the lessons of the past have been lost to so many. Perhaps the Plumbers' crimes under President Nixon have receded so much into history that they are no longer in the minds of today's government and business leaders when they think about what they should or should not do. Or perhaps people have become used to those kinds of crimes, and it takes something sensational to catch the public's attention.

Integrity is threatened in all kinds of competitive institutions. The circumstances, pressures, and incentives may be different between government and other institutions, but the reasons why good people make bad choices are similar.

I am encouraged every day, however, to see the many wonderful and positive people of integrity demonstrating the kind of behavior and decision making I would hope for all of us.

Roy Prosterman, my mentor in land reform, has maintained an unwavering commitment to his cause for more than forty years.

He is a man who identified clearly a whole and complete solution to a specific problem, then went about working for the right and the good.

Jim Ellis, my mentor in public policy in Washington State, continues to provide leadership and guidance so that major public works can be developed that benefit everyone. A leader in cleaning up Lake Washington and in creating a greenway along the I–90 freeway corridor from Seattle through the Cascade Mountains, he also made sure that the Washington State convention center project more than replaced the low-income housing it displaced with a greater number of units of clean, affordable, ultra-low-income housing.

And in the realm of the spiritual, I have had many master teachers who had wonderful influences on me and others. Marianne Williamson in particular and others like her are able to show people a path that enables them to direct themselves into a zone of ethics and adherence to the highest levels of conscience and integrity.

I believe that understanding integrity can guide each of us to the right decisions. Whether in public service or in private business, each of us is presented with difficulties and opportunities. Integrity can show us how to assess, understand, and appropriately react to those circumstances. And with integrity in their hearts, good people in tough circumstances will find themselves making good decisions.

Afterword:
The Integrity Zone

To view the Integrity Zone diagram visit
www.budkrogh.com

To help good people avoid making mistakes like I did, over the last couple of years I have more formally expanded on the ideas set out in my 2001 letter to the Bush staff by creating a model called the "Integrity Zone." The Integrity Zone is based on the idea that every individual has an intrinsic integrity, an inner awareness of what is right and good, commonly called conscience. Living in the Integrity Zone begins with a clear understanding that this quality of integrity inheres in our true selfhood and can be accessed by a desire to be in good conscience. Here is what the Integrity Zone looks like:

At the core of the Integrity Zone, we see the three key questions that we need always to be asking as we carry out our professional and personal activities. The model is a framework of questions, not a menu with answers. In addition to the two questions from the 2001 article (Is it whole and complete? Is it right?), I added a third question: is it good? The first question engages analytical and intellectual reasoning with an objective of ensuring that all relevant aspects of a decision, including second-, third-, and fourth-order consequences, have been considered.

The second question focuses on the moral requirements. Actions need to be in line with core values such as truth, honesty, fairness, respect, responsibility, and compassion.

In my energy law practice, I knew several individuals whose personal lives were severely harmed by the meltdown of their pensions following the collapse of Enron. Enron defendants appeared to have been more concerned about their own enrichment and not the potential effect of their decisions on the lives of their employees. Government and business leaders must constantly consider the consequences of their decisions for the lives of those who are directly affected by them.

The final question, "Is it good?," helps turn our focus to understanding whether an action is beneficial to others. Subsidiary questions are: Is life enhanced? And will this lead to an improvement in the conditions affected by this action? While "do no harm" should be an initial guide to avoid a negative outcome, the positive path is to "reach out to do good."

The Integrity Zone also identifies both the internal and external threats that can pull us out of the zone. Each of the threats identified in the Integrity Zone model appeared in some form during the period from July 15, 1971, when the White House Plumbers group was formed, until Labor Day weekend of 1971, when the covert action against Dr. Fielding was carried out.

Peer pressure, groupthink, pressure to conform? All of us in the SIU were energized by the president's intense national security concerns. We accepted his perspective on the national security threat without question.

High stakes? When the president angrily stated that the Pentagon Papers release and the leak of the U.S. fallback position in the Strategic Arms Limitation Talks were national security threats and would "not be allowed," we felt that we were dealing with the highest stakes.

Secrecy? Each of our decisions was either made in some kind of a vacuum or influenced by data and other decisions made in a vacuum.

Ambiguity of mission? There was little ambiguity about the direction to "stop the leaks." The real ambiguities came from the lack of clarity in the mission of the SIU. While I was focused on preventing further leaks by determining Dr. Ellsberg's mental state and what classified information he might release in the future, E. Howard Hunt was driven by Chuck Colson's imperative to discredit Dr. Ellsberg as an antiwar spokesperson. But I don't think we understood the real goals, or what their impacts might be if we succeeded.

Adversarial climate? While peer pressure and groupthink played a part, we unquestionably had an "us versus them" mentality. Terms like "enemy" and "traitor" were too readily used to describe Dr. Ellsberg and those who were involved with the Pentagon Papers release. This fueled the adversarial intensity within the SIU. During the Vietnam War era, each of the administrations had to deal with a large and growing segment of the American population who disapproved of the war itself and of how we were fighting it. When the SIU was formed, we had explicit orders that our investigative work was to be secret and undercover. The failure of the FBI to help us created a "do it ourselves" ethic and a team mentality.

Dissembling and distortion? Certainly there was direct pressure from Nixon to deal with the leaks. Were his motives represented as solely related to national security? Yes. Did he probably have other strongly political motives as well? Yes.

All of these threats were experienced by the Plumbers while we worked to stop what we believed to be a critical national security leak. What threatens you may be different, however, and I encourage you to examine the Integrity Zone diagram and use it to think about what kinds of threats might be having the greatest impact on your daily life.

Embedded within the Integrity Zone diagram is a list of essential qualities that can insulate us from both internal and external threats to our integrity. These essential qualities—ability/competence, moral courage, selflessness, right motivation, balanced loyalties, intelligence, humility, good judgment, wisdom/understanding of context—are antidotes to the threats we often face. For example, understanding the need to balance properly our loyalties to our leaders and colleagues and to the legal, moral, and spiritual values that should also guide us can prevent our loyalties from becoming skewed and misplaced.

Moral courage can banish the fear of reprisals when we stand up and oppose what we know to be wrong. I have often contemplated how history would have been different if I had demonstrated sufficient moral courage in 1972, right after the Watergate break-in, to go in and tell the president about the Fielding break-in that the Plumbers had carried out in 1971. At that point he was unaware that the Fielding break-in had occurred. If he had been forced to deal with what we had done in 1971, which would have entailed prosecuting those of us who were responsible, there would have been no need for a cover-up or obstruction of justice following Watergate.

Humility is also an essential quality that can help us avoid the predations that so often are a result of decisions driven by arrogance and hubris. When we can accurately define the threats to our integrity, we can overcome them by manifesting the essential qualities that are part of our true nature.

I have left off of the diagram one last example of an external threat—or perhaps an internal threat for some—and that is money. We are all too often swayed in our moral valuations by the ideas of what money can do for us. In the same vein, what about grades and evaluations? Or the influence of peers who don't have your best interests at heart?

The Integrity Zone is not a static diagram, but a system with which to ensure that you are living at the highest level of integrity you can. Use it, adapt the threats to meet your own experience, and then ask yourself the three questions about your decision:

Is it whole and complete?

Is it right?

Is it good?

On the morning of August 8, 1974, members of the White House staff quietly assembled in the East Room to hear President Nixon, surrounded by his devoted family, give his farewell remarks that ended his political career. While I wasn't there (at the time of his talk I was climbing down from the summit of Mt. Rainier via the "Disappointment Cleaver" route), I learned later from friends that it was a sad and somber occasion for all who attended. In his talk, Nixon engaged in some personal self-examination that I feel summed up the reason for his political demise. After acknowledging those staff members who had given so much to their country, thanking those who had stood by him, and expressing his adoration for his saintly mother, he said: "Always remember, others may hate you, but those who hate you don't win unless you hate them, and then you destroy yourself."

To me this comment explained in large measure why Nixon had to resign his office. Hatred is a voracious appetite that consumes those who indulge it. Those of us who committed a crime in 1971 were partly driven by the hatred that the president expressed toward Ellsberg and others who displeased him. The tragedy in this is that Nixon was also capable of the highest vision and execution of the boldest initiatives. His devotion to peace among the nations of the world, which he pursued with idealism and a "ruthless pragmatism," left an enduring legacy that benefits the world order to this day. If only the hatreds had been kept more firmly in check during his presidency, and his better angels—the angels that recognized the saintliness of his mother—had been dominant, the world would be a different and better place today. If only.

Index

PublicAffairs is a publishing house founded in 1997. It is a tribute to the standards, values, and flair of three persons who have served as mentors to countless reporters, writers, editors, and book people of all kinds, including me.

I.F. STONE, proprietor of *I. F. Stone's Weekly*, combined a commitment to the First Amendment with entrepreneurial zeal and reporting skill and became one of the great independent journalists in American history. At the age of eighty, Izzy published *The Trial of Socrates*, which was a national bestseller. He wrote the book after he taught himself ancient Greek.

BENJAMIN C. BRADLEE was for nearly thirty years the charismatic editorial leader of *The Washington Post*. It was Ben who gave the *Post* the range and courage to pursue such historic issues as Watergate. He supported his reporters with a tenacity that made them fearless and it is no accident that so many became authors of influential, best-selling books.

ROBERT L. BERNSTEIN, the chief executive of Random House for more than a quarter century, guided one of the nation's premier publishing houses. Bob was personally responsible for many books of political dissent and argument that challenged tyranny around the globe. He is also the founder and longtime chair of Human Rights Watch, one of the most respected human rights organizations in the world.

·   ·   ·

For fifty years, the banner of Public Affairs Press was carried by its owner Morris B. Schnapper, who published Gandhi, Nasser, Toynbee, Truman, and about 1,500 other authors. In 1983, Schnapper was described by *The Washington Post* as "a redoubtable gadfly." His legacy will endure in the books to come.

Peter Osnos, *Founder and Editor-at-Large*